© Marc Michaels

2009

ISBN 978-0-9810947-6-2
First Edition

The cover photograph shows verses 15:1-11 from *D'varim* beginning at the bottom of one *amud* (column) and then merged into the rest on the next *amud*. This *Torah* contained beautiful *fleur de lys* type *taggin* and I had just repaired this section - hence the shiny letters.
It contains the holy Name of God so please treat it with care.

GIVE!

An analysis of the biblical commandment
to support the poor
with particular reference to the
Tannaitic interpretation
in *Sifre* to *D'varim* 15:7-11

Published by Kulmus Publishing through lulu.com

Copyright © Marc Michaels 2009

The moral right of the author has been asserted.
No part of this publication may be reproduced, stored in a retrieval system
or transmitted in any form or by any means, electronic, mechanical,
photocopying, recording, scanning or otherwise
except under the terms of the Copyright, Designs and Patents Act 1998.

Cover, illustrations and design © Marc Michaels 2009
Typeset in Times New Roman and Frank Ruhl

Contents

Introduction	4
Section 1 - 'in every place'	12
Section 2 - 'do not harden your heart'	33
Section 3 - 'your end will be to take from him'	38
Section 4 - 'even a hundred times'	46
Section 5 - 'to embolden his spirity'	51
Section 6 - 'which is lacking for him'	72
Section 7 - without the yoke'	91
Section 8 - 'seven years for everyone'	101
Section 9 - 'quicker to exact retribution'	106
Section 10 - 'you will surely give'	113
Section 11 - 'the Chamber of Secrets'	114
Section 12 - 'a reward for the saying - a reward for the deed'	121
Section 13 - 'the needy will never cease'	136
Section 14 - 'good counsel I give to you'	142
Section 15 - 'if it is fitting'	145
Overview	150
Appendix 1 - Maimonides 'ladder of *t'sdakah* giving'	156
Bibliography	159

stands for גומל דלים - be kind to the poor.
Why is the foot of the *Gimel* stretched out toward the *Dalet*?
Because a poor person should
make himself available to the rich person.
And why is the *Dalet*'s face turned away from the *Gimel*?
Because the rich should give to the poor discretely,
in order that the poor person not feel ashamed before him.

Shabbat 104a

Introduction

צדקה *ts'dakah*[1] - the giving of charity, or more properly acting righteously to another person to relieve them of the burden of poverty is not merely a 'nice thing to do that gives you a warm fuzzy feeling' as it can be seen in Western society but according to *Torah*, is a duty, indeed a **commandment**.[2]

Much has been written on the subject of *ts'dakah* in Judaism, and the *halachah* (law) in codes such as the *Mishneh Torah* or the *Shulchan Aruch* runs to many pages. Yet, in a similar way to that by which the Rabbis have 'suspended the many laws of the Sabbath on a thread', there is relatively little in the *Torah* about the giving of *ts'dakah*.

One of the main passages that has been used as a basis for much of the development of the law occurs in the portion *Re'eh* in the book of *D'varim*.[3] Here there are five verses which specify how one should deal with the אביון *evyon* (needy person), specifically when the Sabbatical Year is approaching. *D'varim* 15:7-11 reads:

---

1. This is traditionally translated as 'charity' but this does not convey the full meaning of the word צדקה, which is based on the root צדק (righteousness/justice). This implies righteous deeds or just action for which there is an <u>obligation</u> on others towards the poor - see section 2, p.29, note 2. This term will be left untranslated throughout this study.
2. According to the Rambam's (Moses Maimonides, Cordoba, Spain 1135- 1204) list in *Sefer Hamitsvot* (The Book of Commandments) 'to give charity' is number 250.
3. 'A <u>key</u> text is Deuteronomy 15:7-11. In this context the reference is to the 'year of release' the seventh year, when debts were to be cancelled.' (JACOBS, L, *Charity*, from *What Does Judaism Say About...?,* Keter Publishing House, Jerusalem, 1988, p.79.

ז כִּי־יִהְיֶה בְךָ אֶבְיוֹן מֵאַחַד אַחֶיךָ בְּאַחַד שְׁעָרֶיךָ בְּאַרְצְךָ אֲשֶׁר־יְהוָה אֱלֹהֶיךָ נֹתֵן לָךְ לֹא תְאַמֵּץ אֶת־לְבָבְךָ וְלֹא תִקְפֹּץ אֶת־יָדְךָ מֵאָחִיךָ הָאֶבְיוֹן: ח כִּי־פָתֹחַ תִּפְתַּח אֶת־יָדְךָ לוֹ וְהַעֲבֵט תַּעֲבִיטֶנּוּ דֵּי מַחְסֹרוֹ אֲשֶׁר יֶחְסַר לוֹ: ט הִשָּׁמֶר לְךָ פֶּן־יִהְיֶה דָבָר עִם־לְבָבְךָ בְלִיַּעַל לֵאמֹר קָרְבָה שְׁנַת־הַשֶּׁבַע שְׁנַת הַשְּׁמִטָּה וְרָעָה עֵינְךָ בְּאָחִיךָ הָאֶבְיוֹן וְלֹא תִתֵּן לוֹ וְקָרָא עָלֶיךָ אֶל־יְהוָה וְהָיָה בְךָ חֵטְא: י נָתוֹן תִּתֵּן לוֹ וְלֹא־יֵרַע לְבָבְךָ בְּתִתְּךָ לוֹ כִּי בִּגְלַל ׀ הַדָּבָר הַזֶּה יְבָרֶכְךָ יְהוָה אֱלֹהֶיךָ בְּכָל־מַעֲשֶׂךָ וּבְכֹל מִשְׁלַח יָדֶךָ: יא כִּי לֹא־יֶחְדַּל אֶבְיוֹן מִקֶּרֶב הָאָרֶץ עַל־כֵּן אָנֹכִי מְצַוְּךָ לֵאמֹר פָּתֹחַ תִּפְתַּח אֶת־יָדְךָ לְאָחִיךָ לַעֲנִיֶּךָ וּלְאֶבְיֹנְךָ בְּאַרְצֶךָ: ס

Text scanned from *Mikra'ot G'dolot: D'varim*, Pardes Publishing House Inc., New York, 1951

A fairly literal translation of this section would be:

7. If there is a needy man from one of your brothers, in one of your gates, in your land, which the Lord, your God, gives to you, you will not harden your heart and you will not close your hand from your brother the needy.
8. For you will surely open your hand to him and you will surely lend him sufficient from his lack which is lacking to him.[1]
9. Guard yourself, lest there will be a thing with[in] your heart that is *b'lial* (base/evil)[2] saying, the seventh year approaches, the year of *sh'mittah* (release)[3] and your eye be evil against your brother and you do not give to him, and he call against you to God, and there will be sin in you.
10. You will surely give to him and your heart will not be evil in your giving to him, for because of this thing, the Lord your God will bless you in all your deeds and the work [lit. sending] of your hands.
11. For the poor will never cease from the midst of the Earth, therefore I command you saying you will surely open your hand to your brother, to your poor and to your needy [that are] in your land.

There are laws of *ts'dakah* that are not derived from these verses or even from Scripture at all. This book, however, will not concern itself with the whole gamut of issues relating to *ts'dakah*, since that would be far too large an endeavour.

Instead, this study will take a detailed look at these five verses and how

---

1. Often translated as 'enough from that which he needs'. See section 6 for discussion.
2. See section 7 for discussion of this word.
3. As described in *D'varim* 15:1-2,

מקץ שבע־שנים תעשה שמטה: וזה דבר השמטה שמוט כל־בעל משה ידו
אשר ישה ברעהו לא־יגש את־רעהו ואת־אחיו כי־קרא שמטה ליהוה:

(at the end of seven years you will make a release. And this is the manner of the release, every creditor that loans to his neighbour, he will not approach his neighbour or his brother [to collect it] for he has proclaimed a release to the Lord).

they were understood by the Rabbinical authorities who flourished from 20 CE to around 200 CE,[1] known as the *Tannaim*. To this end, particular reference will be made to the insights presented in, arguably 'the oldest juristic commentary',[2] 'the *Midrash* to the book of *D'varim* which is given the designation *Sifre*'.[3]

In form, 'the *Sifre* to Deuternomomy ... is a running exegetical[4] *Midrash* ... expounding the text chapter by chapter and verse by verse ... it is primarily a halakhic *Midrash*'[5] in that its main concern is to extract the legal implications of the Biblical verses. It is difficult to accurately date any Rabbinical text, but 'it is probable that it was arranged and edited in *Erez* Israel but not before the end of the fourth century CE',[6] though much of the material itself dates from earlier periods.

'The work has been traditionally referred to as *Sifre de-be Rav*'[7] and is thought to be 'basically from the school of R. Akiva'[8] though not

---

1. According to Steinsaltz. See STEINSALTZ, A, *The Talmud: A Reference Guide*, Random House, 1989, p.31. Maccoby, however, suggests the period runs from 10 CE to 200 CE, including the pre-destruction Pharisees, but excluding R. Y'hudah Hanasi's younger contemporaries. See MACCOBY, H, *Early Rabbinic Writings*, Cambridge University Press, 1990, p.xx. Strack and Stemberger suggest that the *Tannaim* flourished from 70 CE (i.e. from the destruction of the Temple) and that the authorities that preceed that date form a separate category. See STRACK, H L, & STEMBERGER, G, *Introduction to Talmud and Midrash*, T & T Clark, 1991, p.71-75.
2. MOORE, G F, *Judaism in the First Centuries of the Christian Era: The Age of the Tannaim*, Harvard University Press, Cambridge, 1950, p.165.
3. 'Which is the plural of the Aramaic *Sifra* [(book)] ... [so] used because the *Midrashim* on both Numbers and Deuteronomy appear together as one work'. (HAMMER, R, *Sifre: A Tannaitic Commentary on the Book of Deuteronomy*, Yale University Press, 1986, p.4).
4. See STRACK & STEMBERGER, *op. cit.*, p. 261 for discussion.
5. Encyclopedia Judaica, *Sifrei*, col. 1520.
6. *Ibid.*, col. 1519.
7. HAMMER, *op. cit.*, p.5. Also see *B'rachot* 18b.
8. *Ibid.*, p.8. R. Akiva b. Joseph, 2nd generation *Tanna*. See STRACK & STEMBERGER, *op. cit.*, p.79.

exclusively so.¹

The section that will primarily concern us begins part way through *piska* (paragraph) 116 and ends in *piska* 118, according to the standard numbering utilised in the Finkelstein edition.² It is this critical edition, based on the work of H. S. Horowitz, which will serve as the base text for discussion.

There are, however, many variant texts,³ and also many commentaries and printed editions of the *Sifre*, which will be referred to. Chief amongst these are *Toldot Adam*,⁴ *Emek Han'tsiv*⁵ and that of M. Friedmann.⁶ The two English translations of the work, by Reuven Hammer and Jacob Neusner⁷ have also been consulted. Sadly not all the commentaries that would undoubtedly have proved useful were available for this study.

In order to evaluate the *Sifre* text more fully, many parallel texts and texts containing ideas similar to, or developed from, those presented in *Sifre*, have also been examined, in particular, *Tosefta Pe'ah* chapter 4,

---

1. See *ibid.*, pp.294-298 for full discussion of the character, origins and structure of *Sifre*.
2. Ed. FINKELSTEIN, L, & HOROWITZ, *Sifre on Deuteronomy*, Berlin, 1939, repr. JTSA, New York, 1969. Though both Hammer and Neusner feel that this is 'an eclectic text containing certain emendations' (HAMMER, op. cit., p.xiii), it is the most readily available for study and both have used it as a basis for their own translations. Where there is significant variation in readings, note has been made in this study.
3. Listed in the Finkelstein edition. Also consulted in this area were the הגאות הגר״א (emendations of the GR"A, the Vilna Gaon).
4. ספרי עם פירוש תולדות אדם מאת הגאון רבי משה דוד אברהם טרו׳ש וצ״ל. Mossad Harav Kook, Jerusalem, 1974.
5. ספרי על ספר דברים בשם עמק הנצי״ב מאת נפתלי צבי יהודה ברלין. Jerusalem.
6. *Sifre debe Rab, der älteste halachische und hagadische Midrasch zu Numeri und Deuteronomium*, FRIEDMANN, M, Vienna, 1864.
7. NEUSNER, J, *Sifre to Deuteronomy: An Analytical Translation*, (2 vols), Atlanta, 1987.

Y'rushalmi Pe'ah chapter 8, *Midrash Tannaim*[1] to the same *D'varim* verses, and certain extracts from the Babylonian *Talmud*. Use of these texts has largely been confined to material that appears to stem from the Tannaitic period. Occasional reference will, however, be made to later, largely Amoraic[2] works, Biblical commentators[3] and codes, where these shed light on the earlier works, or where they demonstrate a particular development of the *halachah*.

The base text has been divided into sections related by subject matter,[4] and not necessarily following the standard divisions, or the Biblical verses. A new translation based on a careful study of the text, commentaries, other translations and usage of similar language in parallel texts has been prepared. This is followed by a detailed examination of the content of each section to determine how the *Tannaim* understood the Biblical verse, interpreting it 'against the background of the reality of their own times and environment'.[5]

---

1. Ed. HOFFMAN, D, *Midrasch Tannaim zum Deuteronomium*, Berlin 1908/9 repr. Jerusalem 1984.
2. The Amoraim (lit. 'those who say' or 'those who tell over'), were Jewish scholars who commented on the Oral law, from about 200 to 500 CE in Babylonia and Israel. Their legal discussions and debates were eventually codified in the *Gemara*.
3. In particular Rashi, whose commentary to this section of *Torah* is largely a paraphrase of the *Sifre* text.
4. Though this study has been necessarily arranged in linear fashion, it should be noted that there is much cross referencing between various sections as many of the arguments presented by the *Tannaim* in one area find echoes in other parts of the text.
5. URBACH, E, *The Sages: Their Concepts and Beliefs*, Harvard University Press, 1987. Gerald Bruns notes that, 'what is at issue with respect to the Scriptures is not what lies behind the text in the form of an original meaning but what lies in front of it where the interpreter stands. The Bible always addresses itself to the time of interpretation, one cannot understand it except by appropriating it anew' (BRUNS, G L, *Midrash and Allegory, The Beginnings of Scriptual Interpretation, from, The Literary Guide to the Bible*, Ed. ALTER, R, & KERMODE, F, Collins, 1987, p.267).

This work also tries 'to ascertain what is troubling or inspiring the midrashic author',[1] and look at the way in which this affected the practical application of the *mitsvah* of giving *ts'dakah*.

As Boyarin has written, 'traditional scholarship has considered *Midrash* a wholly transparent reflection of the historical conditions obtaining at the time of its creation ... a kind of historical allegory disguised as pseudohistory'[2] and whilst using Rabbis names as an aid for dating the texts is not wholly reliable,[3] by reference to *Sifre* and many of the parallel texts,[4] the Sages cited tend to be from the third generation of *Tannaim*. This would suggest that the concepts and ideas we will examine stem largely from the period c.130 - 160 CE,[5] during which the Jews witnessed the second uprising against Rome - the Bar Kochba revolt - when 'life became hard with heavy taxation and much poverty'.[6] These events may have been the spur for much of the exegesis seen in our *Sifre* passage. Certainly, when the revolt was over, there was renewed activity on the part of Jewish scholars to define the law.[7]

---

1. HOLTZ, B, *Back to the Sources*, Summit Books, 1984, p.190.
2. BOYARIN, D, *Intertextuality and Midrash*, Indiana University, 1990, p.117.
3. Though 'the study of extensive units has shown that at least in Tannaitic collections, these attributions are largely reliable' (STRACK STEMBERGER, *op. cit.*, pp.63-64. Neusner, however, argues against accepting such ascriptions in his introduction. See NEUSNER, *op. cit.*, p.2-3.
4. The section of *Sifre* text under discussion contains only two named authorities.
5. *Ibid.*, p.83.
6. GRANT, M, *The Jews in the Roman World*, Dorset Press, 1984, p.257.
7. And those pertaining to *ts'dakah* were no exception, as Urbach notes, 'the extent to which the evaluations of the ordinances by the Sages were liable to changes due to social and political circumstances is particularly manifest in their dicta concerning the precept of charity' (URBACH, *op. cit.*, p.348). Hammer explains that 'the challenges of the legitimacy of Judaism were at their height [and] it was important, therefore to strengthen the authority of Rabbinic Law and to demonstrate the divine nature of Scripture by interpreting the legal portions of Deuteronomy in such a way as to integrate the halakah with Scriptural verses' (HAMMER, *op.cit.*, p.16).

Perhaps the *Tannaim* took even greater refuge in the texts, which in turn led to much productivity in learning. Our section of *Sifre* appears to be very much a part of this.[1]

---

1. Whilst it is noted that 'the work of the authorship of *Sifre* to Deuteronomy reaches us through a long process of copying and recopying [and] accordingly we cannot be certain that the Hebrew version in our hands is the one originally sent into the world by the authorship of the document' (NEUSNER, op. cit., p.4), nonetheless it still represents a good statement of what the *Tannaim* wished to say and what they believed and this is generally accepted as such through this study. In order to maintain a consistent approach throughout the study the following conventions have been employed: a) The text under discussion is given in bold at the start of each section; b) English translations of Hebrew text are generally given in brackets ( ), and try to adhere as far as possible to the literal meaning of the words, to convey the economy of the language. Where this would render the translation difficult to understand, linking phrases or explanations are supplied in square brackets [ ]; c) Where Scriptural text is translated within a section of Rabbinic text, this is given in single inverted commas within the translation ' '. The translation given does not necessarily correspond with how the Sages may have subsequently interpreted it; d) Hebrew words or phrases translated once are generally not translated again when they occur more than once within a section; e) Hebrew words that are not quotations are given in transliteration, e.g. *Midrash*, *Tanna*, excluding roots of verbs that are shown in Hebrew characters. Transliterations are consistent through the body of the study, but may differ from transliterations as they appear in quotations from secondary sources. Similarly, transliterated Hebrew words are shown in italics in the body of the study, but may not be in a quotation from a secondary source where italics were not employed; f) The Hebrew names for the Biblical or Rabbinical texts are generally used rather than any Latin equivalents, i.e. *D'varim* rather than Deuteronomy, unless in quotation from a secondary source.

Section 1 - 'in every place'

כי יהיה בך ולא באחרים **אביון** תאב תאב קודם **אחיך** זה אחיך מאביך כשהוא אומר מאחד אחיך מלמד שאחיך מאביך קודם לאחיך מאמך **באחד שעריך** יושבי עירך קודמים ליושבי עיר אחרת **בארצך** יושבי הארץ קודמים ליושבי חוצה לארץ כשהוא אומר באחד שעריך היה יושב במקום אחד אתה מצוה לפרנסו היה מחזר על הפתחים אי אתה זקוק לו לכל דבר אשר ה׳ נתן לך בכל מקום

('If there will be amongst you'. and not amongst others. 'A needy person', [suggesting that] he who needs [the most] takes precedence. 'Your brother', this is the brother from your father, because it [Scripture] says 'from one of your brothers', teaching that your brother from your father takes precedence over your brother from your mother. 'In one of your gates', the inhabitants of your city take precedence over the inhabitants of another city. 'In your land', the inhabitants of the Land [of Israel] take precedence over those who dwell outside the Land. When it says 'in one of your gates', [it teaches that if] he was dwelling in one place, you are commanded to support him. [If] he was going about the the doors [begging], you are not obligated to him for anything. 'Which the Lord gives to you', [implying] in every place.)

This first section of our *midrash* is concerned with establishing who is entitled to receive *ts'dakah* from the individual or the community. This represents an important and practical application of *halachah* for the Rabbis; since the resources of the community would have been limited, whilst the occasions for giving *ts'dakah*, (particularly in the harsh economic circumstances in the 3rd Century, after the Bar Kochba revolt), would have been limitless.[1]

The immediate focus in the *Sifre* interpretation of *D'varim* 15:7 is not, however, on the אביון (needy person), rather it is on the word בך (amongst you). Indeed, in some manuscripts, כי יהיה (if there will be) is not even quoted.[2]

To this word, the *Tannaim* immediately add ולא באחרים (and not amongst others). This is a logical corollary,[3] but somewhat redundant given the Biblical context of the passage, that of Moses addressing the Children of Israel. This would hardly need further amplification. What then is the reason behind the Rabbis' exegesis here?

The most likely explanation is that it is representative of the particularistic viewpoint of the *Tannaim*. It is brought to emphasise that

---

1. Dating the majority of the ideas presented in this passage of *Sifre* to 3rd generation *Tannaim*. See the introduction. The Bar Kokhba revolt in 132-136 CE against the Roman Empire was the third major rebellion by the Jews of Judea Province and the last of the Jewish-Roman Wars. Shim'on bar Kokhba ('son of a star' - though his real name was bar Koziba) was the commander of the revolt and was acclaimed as a Messiah. The revolt established a Jewish state over parts of Judea for over two years, but was finally crushed by the Romans.
2. It is a shame that this is the case, as we have no clarification of their understanding of the meaning of כי here. The word itself in context could be either 'when' or 'if', (see BROWN, DRIVER, BRIGGS, GESENIUS, *Hebrew English Lexicon of the Old Testament*, Hendrickson, 1979, p.473) the former suggesting an inevitability, 'because there will be poor ...' therefore this is the action you need to take. Taking the latter, however, we note that 'כי [can have] a force approximating to 'if' though it usually represents a case as more likely to occur than 'אם (*ibid.*) and this would suggest that there is at least a possibility that there will not be poor amongst you. See later discussions on אפס כי לא יהיה וגו' and כי לא יחדל וגו' (Section 13).
3. For example, commenting on the *M'chilta* to *Sh'mot* 15:2, Boyarin notes that 'if there is a "my" then it seems that there is a "not yours" ... it is hardly surprising then that the *Midrash* understands "This is my God" to imply a rhetorical or dramatic situation in which Israel is addressing some other nation and saying "This is my God" and not yours.' (BOYARIN, D, *Inter-textuality and Midrash*, Indiana University, 1990, p.121).

Jews are only responsible for poverty that occurs <u>within the community of Israel</u> (i.e. other Jews) and not amongst other nations, with whom they, according to *Sifre*, apparently need not be concerned.

אחרים, is also a word that is open to interpretation. Is it simply 'others', or does it imply a stronger form? Neusner gives 'outsiders' in his analytical translation[1] and it is often used pejoratively in Rabbinical writings to refer to the stranger or the gentile.[2] Nowhere in this section of our *Sifre* text, and indeed elsewhere in Tannaitic thought, is there any cause to believe that Jews are <u>obliged</u> to support the poor of other nations.[3] Indeed, when, in other texts, such an 'obligation' is proposed it is out of other motives.[4]

Alternatively, as noted, בך in the context of Moses' speech is directed at Israel as a communal entity,[5] thus validating the Rabbinic conception

---

1. NEUSNER, op. cit., p.290.
2. JASTROW, M, *Dictionary of the Targumim, Talmud Babli, Yerushalmi and Midrashic Literature*, Judaica Press, New York, 1989, p.41.
   Where the phrase כי יהיה בך ולא באחרים is employed in *Sifre Piska* 255, Finkelstein notes that ואין הנכרים מטמאין בקרי מן התורה (and according to Scripture no foreigner can defile from their seminal emmisions) (FINKELSTEIN, *op. cit.*, p.280 from *Niddah* 34a), indicating that אחרים, in that instance at least, refers to foreigners, and the same may be true of its appearance in *Piska* 116.
3. For example, in *Tosefta Pe'ah* 4: 1, we learn that,
   עניי כותים כעניי ישראל אבל עניי גוים אין מאמנים להם בכל דבר (the poor of the *Kutim* [Samaritan sect] [are to be treated] as the poor of Israel (i.e. they are supported) but the poor of the nations, we do not believe them in anything [they say (i.e their claims to poverty]). It is interesting in itself that the *Kutim* are not counted as 'others' or 'outsiders' when it comes to giving *ts'dakah*.
4. *Gittin* 61a states, מפרנסים עניי נכרים עם עניי ישראל ... מפני דרכי שלום (we support the poor of the heathen [along] with the poor of Israel ... <u>for the sake of the ways of peace</u>). A welcome development, even if not from the best of motives!
5. כי יהיה בך אביון can only be said with any decisiveness to a community: One cannot say to an individual as such "if there is a poor man amongst you." (HIRSCH, S R, *The Pentateuch, Vol. 5, Deuteronomy*, 2nd Ed. (rendered into English by I. LEVY), London, 1965, p.269).

of charity as a 'contribution from every citizen towards a common obligation'.¹ Yet, because of its singular form, it also speaks of personal, individual responsibility.² ולא באחרים is perhaps stated to emphasise that the maintenance of these poor is both Israel's personal and collective responsibility and not the responsibility of others. Israel should not rely on the good will of others to support their own poor.

We have thus far read the phrase as fairly neutral in tone. It may, however, be a comment made within the context of an earlier, related *Piska* from *Sifre*, wherein we read,

בזמן שאתם עושים רצונו של מקום אביונים באחרים כשאין אתם עושים רצונו של מקום אביונים בכם

(at a time that you [i.e. Israel] are doing the will of the Omnipresent [lit. the Place], needy people will be amongst others, but when you do not do the will of the Omnipresent, needy people will be amongst you).³

Given this, the reference ולא באחרים could be seen as an accusation of sorts, even an admonishment, to stress that if there were poor amongst Israel, it follows that they have not carried out the will of God and therefore the poor are בכם (amongst you (pl.)) or even בך. The statement ולא באחרים could simply be read as an indictment of failure to give.

All three of the above suggestions see בך as referring to Jews, and אחרים to non-Jews. Elsewhere in Rabbinic literature, however, both references are seen as referring to Jews. בך is instead read in the singular, to imply supporting oneself before other Jews. *Midrash Tannaim* renders, ת"ל כי יהיה בך אביון את קודם לאחרים (Scripture says 'for there will be amongst you a needy [person, implying that] you

---

1. EPSTEIN, I, *Introductory Essay to Bava M'tsia*, Soncino Hebrew-English Ed., Soncino Press, 1986, p.ix.
2. As Hirsch suggests 'the duty of caring and providing for the poor ... rests both on the community and equally every single member of it.' (HIRSCH, *op. cit.*, p.269).
3. *Piska* 114, also in *Piska* 118. See section 13 for discussion.

take precedence over others).[1] This is further developed by the *Amoraim*,[2] which leads Rashi to comment that בך implies that הזהר מן העניות ([you] protect [yourself] from poverty).[3]

Regardless of our precise understanding of בך or אחרים, it is clear that the responsibility to give in the cases that follow lies with Israel, either singly or collectively. This established, only then do the *Tannaim* turn their attention to the recipient.

There are a number of words for a poor person used in Biblical Hebrew, amongst them עני (poor, as in afflicted, humble), דל (poor, as in sparseness), as well as the אביון, as cited in *D'varim* 15:7. For the *Tannaim*, the use of this specific word as opposed to any other would have prompted them to derive a further lesson.

Jastrow[4] indicates that אביון is derived from אבי (to press, surround), possibly suggesting that this form of poverty is like a pressure or a weight upon the poor person. In *Vayikra Rabbah* 34:6, we are informed that, אביון שמתאב לכל ([he is called] *evyon*, because he has a need for everything).[5] *Targum Onkelos* translates as מסכנא (the one of

---

1. *Midrash Tannaim* to *D'varim* 15:7.
2. אמר רב יהודה אמר רב אפס כי לא יהיה בך אביון שלך קודם לשל כל אדם
   (R. Y'hudah said in Rav's name 'Howbeit that there be no poor amongst you' ['amongst you' implying that] yourself takes precedence over others). It is interesting to note that whilst this interpretation was given, it was not necessarily seen as a good thing since the text then adds,
   ואמר רב יהודה אמר רב כל המקיים בעצמו כך סוף לידי כך (but R. Y'hudah [further] said in Rav's name [that] one who practices this [only] for him self, will eventually be brought to this [state of poverty] (*Bava M'tsia* 33a)). See also *Sanhedrin* 64b.
3. Rashi to *Bava M'tsia* 33a. The Soncino Hebrew-English Ed. also notes that the Rabbis were 'regarding this verse as an exhortation against bringing oneself to poverty' (*Bava M'tsia* 30b, note a(l)).
4. JASTROW, *op. cit.*, p.5.
5. This is part of a section where the five names of the poor are given with explanation.

scanty resource),[1] and we learn elsewhere that he is called מסכן שהוא מסוכן בחיין (*misken* because his life is in danger [i.e. he might starve because of lack of resources]).[2] One gets the sense through all this that to be classified as an אביון implies quite a <u>serious level of poverty</u>. Similarly in *Midrash Tannaim* to *D'varim* 15:7, we are told that,

אביון שהוא רואה דבר ואינו אוכל רואה דבר ואינו שותה תאיב לכל

[he is called] *evyon* because he sees a thing but does not eat, sees a thing but does not drink, he requires everything), which also suggests a certain degree of <u>helplessness</u> inherent in this category of poor.

Despite its apparent severity it also seems to imply a relatively temporary state that can be effectively tackled (though perhaps not completely eradicated - see section 13) and many of the examples in this *Sifre* passage centre around the בן טובים (son of good [family]); someone who has fallen on hard times.[3]

In our *midrash* too, the *Tannaim* are keen to point out that this is a case of need[4] by the use of תאב (to want, desire), but go further, suggesting that the use of the word אביון teaches us that the <u>most needy</u> always takes precedence. This statement would seem to indicate that the priority of poor relief was based on individual need and circumstance, which mirrors the ideas explored later about matching the *ts'dakah* given to that which a person lacks.[5] The אביון has probably attained this temporary status of most needy precisely because they appear to be someone who has fallen suddenly and possibly unexpectedly into severe hardship (perhaps through economic or natural disaster from a

---

1. *Ibid.*, p.807.
2. *Midrash Mishley* 22.
3. As opposed to an עני (poor person) which perhaps indicates a more permanent situation; that one is born into.
4. Which perhaps mirrors the use of חסר (lack) later in the text (*D'varim* 15:8), since what is missing is needed by the אביון.
5. See section 6.

previously lofty position. Unused to dealing with this, this kind of poor person is naturally more helpless than someone born to a life of poverty.

In a way this has echoes in our modern society where a sudden disaster, such as a flood or earthquake or even global economic factors can strike an otherwise viable community and this can temporarily eclipse other giving priorities. Perhaps this is why the our passage (*D'varim* 15:11) states that the אביון, in particular, will never cease from the world, as even the best organised communities with full employment, sensible benefit systems and structured charity giving will still see a new set of needy created by a natural or man-made[1] disaster.

However, having established this as a proposition, the *Tannaim* then proceed to introduce a potential conflict by imposing an apparently non-needs-based constraining structure on this - a 'pecking order' of sorts.

It is clearly the tri-partite structure of *D'varim* 15:7, which reads, מאחד אחיך באחד שעריך בארצך (from one of your brothers, in one of your gates, in your land), coupled with the use and repetition of אחד (one), that provoked, or perhaps allowed, the Rabbis to define this hierarchy.

In a characteristically atomistic way,[2] instead of reading the verse as referring to one person, (i.e. 'one of your brothers who lives within your gates within your land') - the *p'shat* (straightforward, literal or

---

1. Such as wars or economic crises that periodically affect the whole world or particular countries that cause massive disruption in the fabric of a society affecting millions.
2. 'The verse centredness of *midrash* ... may reflect the way Scripture was actually taught by the Rabbis, and it is exemplified by their midrashic habit of atomizing the biblical text, breaking up a verse into tinier units and mining its separate phrases and words for meanings.' (STERN, D, *Midrash*, from, Ed. COHEN, A, & MENDES FLOHR, P, *Contemporary Jewish Religious Thought*, Free Press, New York, 1988, p.615).

plain) rendering of the text - they dissect the verse reading each element as totally separate in order to extract a practical lesson.

The first priority, as one would expect, is to support one's own family. This, though, is presented as a given, since the concern of the *Tannaim* is to demonstrate priority <u>within</u> the family itself. How this is established can be seen by examining closely the meaning that the Sages attach to the words אחיך (your brother) and/or אחד (one).

Elsewhere in *Sifre* the *Tannaim* have shown that אחיך refers specifically to the son of your father, i.e. your paternal brother. In their exegesis of כי יסיתך אחיך בן אמך (if you are enticed secretly [to serve other gods] by your brother, the son of your mother)[1] they argue that this refers to two different individuals since,

אחיך זה אחיך מאביך בן אמך זה בן אמך ('your brother' - this is your brother from your father. 'Son of your mother', this is the son of your mother).[2] Assuming there is some degree of internal consistency within *Sifre*,[3] when in our passage the reference is to אחיך (your brother), it is similarly understood as אחיך מאביך (your brother from your father)

Alternatively, the stress may be on אחד. As opposed to 'one', it could be read as 'first'.[4] The Rabbis may have understood the word as implying the first, or most important of your brothers, which would be your paternal brother. Certainly Neusner, whose translation marks *'one of'*, in italics[5] may have had this reasoning, in mind.

---

1. *D'varim* 13:7.
2. *Piska* 87.
3. 'We should note that it is characteristic of *Sifre D.*, that particular interpretative phrases are connected to a specific word or phrase and are then repeated whenever that word appears' (HAMMER, *op. cit.*, p.15).
4. For example in *B'reshit* 1:5 the phrase יום אחד could be taken to mean 'one day' or 'the first day'.
5. NEUSNER, *op, cit.*, p.290.

The commentary *Toldot Adam* suggests that the use of אחד implies for the Sages, המיוחד שבאחיך הוא מן האב (the special one, that is your brother from your father),[1] whilst Malbim argues that the reference is to one who is מאוחדת (united [in inheritance]),[2] again suggesting the paternal brother who would share the inheritance.

In a patriarchal society where property went through the paternal line, your paternal brother would have no other property other than that which you shared with him. The maternal brother, however, could potentially draw on different property arrangements through his fathers line. Thus the 'brother from your father' would have first call on your *ts'dakah* funds.[3]

Having set the form of the exegesis for the verse, the *Sifre* text continues to add further <u>limiting</u> clauses, that the inhabitants of your city take precedence over other cities and those who dwell in Israel take precedence over the Jewish poor from other countries. This <u>narrowing</u> of the scope of giving, provided a framework of legislation and a hierarchy of obligation, which most likely suited the economic circumstance of the time, where funds were very limited and poverty extensive. The need to classify is important as the relative status of the אביון will determine what he or she was entitled to from the communal charity funds.

---

1. *Toldot Adam* s.v. מאחד אחיך.
2. Malbim to *D'varim* 15:7.
3. Regardless of which brother is given precedence, there is still the clear statement by the Rabbis that priority should be given to members of one's family. *N'darim* 65b states that כל הנופל אינו נופל לידי גבאי תחילה (any who fall [into poverty] should not fall into hands of the overseer [of charity] first), instead 'the friends and relations have first to see what they can do and only where that does not suffice does the community make the deficiency up' (HIRSCH, *op. cit.*, p.272). Rambam later develops this, stating that one should first give to the עני שהוא קרובו (poor, that is the closest to him [i.e. a relative] (*Mishneh Torah: Hilchot Mat'not Aniyim* (Laws of gifts to the Poor) 7:13)).

It is arguable however, whether the exegesis here represents the <u>actual practice</u> of the time or is an <u>exhortation</u> by the Rabbis for Jews to follow such practice.

It may be easily argued that giving precedence to your local poor and then to those of inside the land was common practice, determined by geography, if nothing else. The people would most likely expect to look to their own community's welfare first and then that of their own homeland, and the *Tannaim* are using Scripture to support the status quo.[1] In comparison with the other two lessons, however, the exegesis of אחד seems a little contrived. The positioning of the brothers in the hierarchy may have been forced into the verse, either in support of actual practice or, perhaps as a means by which the *Tannaim* wished to shape practice into an agreed form, since they understood that with inheritance laws as they were, this brother would be the one most likely to need support.

More importantly, however, the positing of an hierarchy[2] of giving does seem to be in conflict with the idea they present initially that one gives to תאב תאב קודם (the neediest one first). This may represent a <u>change of emphasis</u> whereby the Jews in post Bar Kochba, devastated Israel,

---

1. Much *halachah*, such as is found in *Mishnah* and the *Tosefta*, is not supported by a textual base unlike *Sifre* and other halachic *Midrashim*. Thus any law could have been derived independently of Scripture through reference to ancient tradition or current practice and the Scriptural basis applied retrospectively, That this is the case is witnessed by the *G'mara*, where one frequently encounters the phrase מאי קראה (what is the Scriptural basis?).
2. Another Tannaitic hierarchy of giving does appear in *M'chilta Mishpatim* 19:3, derived from the words את עני עמך (the poor with you (*Sh'mot* 22:24)), though the relative priority of ones brothers is not mentioned, replaced instead with the idea of putting one's immediate family first,

   ... ענייך ועני עירך ענייך קודמין לעני עירך עני עירך וענייי עיר אחרת עני עירך קודמין

   (... your poor [i.e. your family] and the poor of your city, your poor take precedence, the poor of your city and the poor of another city, the poor of your city take precedence). See *Bava M'tsia* 71a for similar.

are becoming more concerned with communal self-preservation. They may therefore be interpreting the verse anew to limit previous practice which may have been based on an earlier tradition that the neediest were first whoever and wherever they might be. Alternatively we could argue that the two ideas are not mutually exclusive and that having applied the lessons of the hierarchy one then looks for the neediest within that category of poor, for example, having been informed that you give first to the poor of your own city, you then select the neediest amongst those poor. Regardless of any attempt we might make at reconciling the views, there appears to be some tension between the two ideas.

Indeed the verse could have been read differently, not merely as determining preference, but rather to suggest complete exclusion. *Bava M'tsia* 31b poses the question, ... פתח תפתח אין לי אלא לעניי עירך ('you will surely open', I know this only of the poor of your city ...), suggesting that one might literally read באחד שעריך as 'in one of your gates [only]'. However this text immediately demonstrates a more widening stance by adding,

... לעניי עיר אחרת מנין ת״ל פתח תפתך מכל מקום (... from where [do we learn one gives] to the poor of another city, Scripture says 'you will surely open',[1] [implying] from every place [regardless of where they come].

In neither case then does it exclude, but there is an emphasis of limitation in *Sifre* which is not present in the more positive statement from the *G'mara*. In their exegesis then, the *Tannaim* of *Sifre* were apparently promoting a slightly more negative sounding insular approach.[2]

---

1. The use of the absolute form here is typically interpreted as having a meaning over and above a grammatical construction. Instead, it is seen as indicating an extension of the giving to all, in the sense of 'open', to the poor of your own city and also, 'you will open' to the poor of other cities. See section 4 for discussion of the use of this form in the *Sifre* passage.
2. This does not mean that they were somehow at fault or being mean, but perhaps

Despite the order of preference in the phrasing they employ, it does not, however, obviate one's obligation to give to the poor of other cities or to those of other countries. This is perhaps further supported by the *Sifre* interpretation of אשר ה' אלקיך נתן לך ('which the Lord your God gives you').[1] The comment בכל מקום (in all places), is translated by Neusner[2] as 'anywhere', which would tend to echo the idea of a wider stance in giving, in that we are obliged to give to the poor wherever we find them, אף בחוצה לארץ (even outside the Land [of Israel]),[3] and this appears to be the accepted view.

This leads us in turn to another area of difficulty with the text. Since the principle of giving to those outside the Land has <u>already</u> been assumed by the hierarchy, (even though these poor would come last in the list), what then does the statement בכל מקום really add?

---

were being realistic, given the prevailing conditions. That they were still prepared to sacrifice much to *ts'dakah* is witnessed by a different interpretation of בשעריך (within your gates (*D'varim* 14:29)). *Piska* 110 states,

מלמד שאין מוציאים אותו מן הארץ לחוצה לארץ אמרו משפחת בית נבלטה היתה בירושלים ונתנו להם שש מאות ככרי זהב ולא רצו להוציא חוץ לירושלים (hence we learn that the poor may not be removed from the Land to outside the Land. They said [that when] the family of the house of Nebalta was [living] in Jerusalem they gave them six hundred talents of gold [as] they did not want them to leave Jerusalem). If the poor did leave they would cease to be a burden on the community but nonetheless their stated aim, both generally and in the case cited, is to keep them.

1. *D'varim* 15:7.
2. NEUSNER, *op. cit.*, p.290.
3. Supported by the idea that,

גורס בסמ"ג בהדיא יושבי חוצה לארץ מנין דכתיב אשר ה' אלקיך נתן לך כל מקום

(it reads in the *Sefer Mitsvot Gadol* explicitly, from where [do we learn that we give to] those who dwell outside the Land, it is written, 'which the Lord your God gives to you' - [implying] everywhere) (FINKELSTEIN, *op. cit.*, p.175).

Toldot Adam suggests that it is still related to the hierarchy,[1] but that,

עם יושב בח"ל ועניי עירו א"י א"י קודמין ושיעור הכתוב בארצך עניי ארץ ישראל אשר ה' אלהיך נתן לך בכל מקום הם קודמים

(if one dwells outside the Land and [it is a choice between] poor of one's city and the poor of the Land of Israel, the Land of Israel takes precedence and the lesson of Scripture 'in your land' [is that the] poor of the Land of Israel, 'which the Lord your God gives you' in all places [meaning <u>instances</u> rather than geographical location] they are first). This would imply that the Israel-centred *Tannaim* of *Sifre* were considering the case of one whose city was outside Israel. This seems unlikely, though it is possible given the increased emigration at that time.[2]

Hammer, however, appears to relate בכל מקום to the case of the beggar at the door (see below), translating it as 'wherever that may be',[3] in that you <u>do not give</u> to such a person regardless of whether it is in your city, in Israel or elsewhere.

Finally, בכל מקום could mean 'at every opportunity', i.e. in all places that the opportunity to perform the *mitsvah* presents itself. *The Tannaim* may be drawing here on the use in the verse of נותן (gives). The present tense perhaps indicates a constant giving on the part of God, which would therefore be reflected by a <u>constant</u> giving of *ts'dakah* by Israel.

That the verb has been noted by the *Tannaim* is shown by the presence in some manuscripts of a misreading of the Torah verse as

---

1. And that the section addressing the problem of one who מחזר על הפתחים (goes about the doors [begging]) is a later interpolation.
2. 'The revolts disastrous end created a real danger of mass emigration for the first time. The fears raised by this threat are explicitly expressed in the writings of the Palestinian Sages who thereby formulated the obligations of the Jews in regard to the Land of Israel' (BARNARVI, E, *A Historical Atlas of the Jewish People*, Hutchinson, 1992, p.61).
3. HAMMER, *op. cit.*, p.161.

אשר ה׳ אלקיך יתן לך (which the Lord your God will give you). Aside from being a correction of the chronology (God had not, at that point, given the Israelites the Land of Israel), this could indicate that the Sages deliberately misread this to imply that God would only give the Israelites the Land, if they gave to the poor.

As noted briefly above, before the comment בכל מקום, the *Sifre* text also supplies an additional comment to באחד שעריך (in one of your gates). Once again, the *Tannaim* see a special significance in the word אחד and suggest that it can be read as a needy person who resides in one place only, as opposed to one who is apparently transient. Certainly the *halachah* indicates that certain funds that were available to support someone who resides in your city were not available for the itinerant.[1]

This bias is probably due to the prevailing opinion amongst the Rabbis that it is better for a person not to rely on charity, and that the highest degree of charity is to help someone achieve this.[2] This would require a person to put down roots and may be reflected by the use of לפרנסו (to support him) in the Rabbinic texts, which also conveys a sense of growth and cultivation,[3] perhaps to emphasise the need to make the

---

1. תמחוי לכל אדם קופה לעניי אותה העיר (The *tamchui* [charity plate] is for everyone, the *kuppah* [communal fund (lit. basket)] is for the poor of that city (*Tosefta Pe'ah* 4:9)).
2. This principle is later stated by Rambam as,

   מעלה גדולה שאין למעלה ממנה זה המחזיק ביד ישראל שמך ונותן לו
   מתנה או הלואה או עושה עמו שתפות או ממציא לו מלאכה כדי לחזק את
   ידו עד שלא יצטרך לבריות לשאל

   (the greatest level [of *ts'dakah*] that there is none higher than, is to strengthen the hand of the Israelite that became poor and give to him a gift or a loan, or make a partnership with him or find him work, in order to strengthen his hand, until he does not need to ask of anyone (*Mishneh Torah: Hilchot Mat'not Aniyim* 10:7)). See Appendix 1.
3. JASTROW, *op. cit.*, p.1281

אביון self sufficient.[1]

Given limited resources it would also be unfair to expect a community to have to support vagrants from other cities as well as their own, since the poor would tend to congregate in those cities whose inhabitants were the most generous.

The key to this section, however, is how the *Tannaim* feel about מחזר על הפתחים (one who goes about the doors [begging]). Hammer notes that although *Sifre* implies that we are not obligated to give to such a person, 'in other sources it is stated that one must still give him a small sum, such as is given to any other needy person'.[2] This may be why Neusner translates לכל דבר as 'in every little thing'[3] suggesting that you do give him some small thing but not <u>every</u> thing he asks for. But a more accurate reading of the phrase, arguably is that, literally אי אתה זקוק לו לכל דבר (you are not obligated to him for <u>anything</u>).

The first text which Hammer brings in support of his view is *Tosefta Pe'ah* 4:8 but this actually states that though,

אין פותחין לעני העובר ממקום למקום מככר בפונדיון מארבע סאין בסלע

(we do not give less to the poor [person] who passes from place to place than a loaf costing a *pondion*[4] when four *se'ahs*[5] [measures of flour] cost a *sela*[6]) when it refers thereafter to our specific case, it still

---

1. 'There is always a danger that instead of alleviating distress, [*ts'dakah*] might destroy the character of the recipient ... it is for this reason that the poor had ... to work for what had been assigned to them as their share, and thus maintain their sense of self respect' (EPSTEIN, *op. cit.*, p.ix).
2. HAMMER, *op. cit.*, p.438, note 5.
3. NEUSNER, *op. cit.*, p.290.
4. A copper coin with which you could buy a loaf of bread. See CARMELL, A, *Aiding Talmud Study*, Feldheim Publishers, 1991, p83.
5. A *se'ah* is a unit of dry volume which is approximately equal to 7.33 litres.
6. A silver coin that was the Rabbinical equivalent of the Biblical *shekel*. It could buy you rent of a dwelling for a month. See CARMELL, *ibid.*

concludes, היה מסביב על הפתחים אין נזקקין לו בכל דבר ([if] he was going about the doors [begging], we are not obligated to him in anything).[1]

This seems to indicate that for the *Tannaim*, one who was going ממקום למקום (from place to place) was substantively different from one who מחזר על הפתחים (goes about the doors [begging]). The former, travelling from town to town, would not be able to benefit from the communal funds and thus would need to be given some small sustenance. The latter, however, would be a resident and thus eligible. The objection against the beggar, raised in *Sifre*, seems not that he was undeserving because he was a 'transient' poor person, rather it was because he was trying to act outside of the formal organised, and therefore legitimate, collective system of charity dispensation, which was favoured by the Rabbis.[2] Such a person would be acting on an individual basis trying to get more than his share by exploiting the goodwill of the inhabitants of his town.

Aside from this action being outside the favoured system, the *Tannaim* most likely regarded begging as a particularly low form[3] of *ts'dakah* since it was damaging from the point of view of both the recipient and the donor; the recipient, because his dignity is all but gone as he has to open the transaction, and the donor who is more or less accosted and would find it difficult to refuse.[4] Those who went from door to door

---

1. Similar is to be found in *Y'rushalmi Pe'ah* 4: 8.
2. Moore notes that 'public provision ... being made, begging from door to door was disfavoured; charitable housewives often gave food to such mendicants, but the latter then forfeited their rights to assistance from the overseers of the poor' (MOORE, *op. cit.*, p.177). Whilst Hirsch is somewhat critical of the stance 'no beggars need apply, the owners subscribe generously to public funds' (HIRSCH, *op. cit.*, p.270), this is nonetheless a fair description of the Tannaitic viewpoint in this case.
3. Rambam posited eight levels of *ts'dakah* giving. See Appendix 1 for details.
4. Epstein note that 'by these means [i.e. the well organised charity institutions] the degrading system of house-to-house visitation was considerably obviated' (EPSTEIN, *op. cit.*, p.ix).

would not have met the key requirement of *kavod* (honour) in the act of giving and receiving, that was important to the Rabbis and would instead have been a source of *bushah* (shame) for both parties.[1] Such discomfort is still evident, even today.[2]

These views perhaps explain the fairly harsh treatment of such a person by R. Chiyya[3] at the end of the Tannaitic period. Despite maintaining that when a poor person comes to the door one should be quick to give because of the negative consequences of not doing so,[4] his subsequent actions do not reflect his own advice. Instead,

אמרה ליה מילט קא לייטת להו (she [his wife] said to him [Chiyya] you [i.e. Chiyya, do not give to them, instead you] curse them).[5] An Amoraic Sage, R. Yosef,[6] supports the antipathy towards this mode of seeking charity, by exclaiming that,

אהדורי אפתחא לא מיהדר אם איתא דמיעני (even if he [a Rabbinical student] suffers poverty, he should not engage in going about the doors [begging]).[7]

In contrast to the hierarchy of giving, which may be partly an example of Scripturally derived practice, trying to impress a pattern on the community, what we have here seems likely to be an agreed practice which the Rabbis in *Sifre* were able to further legitimise by positing Scriptural derivation from באחד שערך.

---

1. See section 5 for discussion of *bushah* (shame).
2. For example 'chugging', the practice of so-called 'charity mugging' whereby members of the public are approached on the street or on their doorstep by a paid charity fundraiser who attempts to get them to sign up to make regular monthly donations.
3. R. Chiyya bar Abba (Chiyya I), a 5th generation *Tanna*. See STRACK & STEMBERGER, *op. cit.*, p.90.
4. i.e. *galgal*, the turning of the wheel which means that he or his descendents would eventually suffer poverty if they were not to give (see section 3).
5. *Shabbat* 151b.
6. R. Yosef bar Chiyya, a 3rd generation Babylonian *Amora*. See STRACK & STEMBERGER, *op. cit.*, p.102.
7. *Shabbat* 151b.

Indeed, there does not appear to be a discernable movement away from this somewhat strict attitude of the *Tannaim* until late in the Amoraic period, as reported in *Y'rushalmi Pe'ah* 8: 6 and in *Bava Batra* 9a. The former text indicates a dissension from the *Sifre* view[1] by the *Amora* R. Yonah,[2] who argues, that the Tannaitic view holds, ובלחוד דלא יפחות ליה מן ארגרון דיליה (provided that you do not refuse him his customary *argyron* [a small silver coin known as the beggar's penny[3]]). Bava Batra reports an actual case,

ההוא עניא דהוה מחזיר על הפתחים דאתא לקמיה דרב פפא לא מזדקיק ליה א"ל רב סמא בריה דרב ייבא לרב פפא אי מר לא מזדקיק ליה אינש אחרינא לא מזדקיק ליה, לימות ליה והא תניא אם היה עני המחזיר על הפתחים אין נזקקין לו א"ל אין נזקקין לו למתנה מרובה, אבל נזקקין לו למתנה מועטת

(a certain poor man who went around the doors [begging] came before R. Papa.[4] He did not give to him. R. Sama, son of R. Yeyba said to R.Papa, if the master [i.e. Papa] does not feel obliged to give to him, no-one else will feel obliged to give to him. Should he [then] die? But [replied R. Papa] is it not taught that if there was a poor man who went around the doors [begging], we are not obligated to him for anything. He [R. Sama] said to him [R. Papa] we are not obligated to him for a large gift, but we are obligated to him for a small gift).[5]

---

1. Which appears in this case phrased in the plural,
תני המסבבין על הפתחים אין נזקקים להן לכל דבר (it has been taught [by a *Tanna* that] those who go around the doors [begging], we are not obligated to them for anything).
2. A 5th generation Palestinian Amora, head of the academy of Tiberias. See STRACK & STEMBERGER, *op. cit.*, p.105.
3. JASTROW, *op. cit.*, p.115.
4. R. Papa ben Chanan, a 5th generation Babylonian *Amora*. See STRACK & STEMBERGER, *op. cit.*, p.106. *Tosafot* to *Bava Batra* 9a notes,
רב פפא גבאי היה ולא נתן לו מן הקופה כדתניא אין נותנין לו (Rav Papa was a [charity] collector and did not give to him from the *kuppah*, as it is taught [in the *baraita*]we do not give him).
5. 'i.e, something less than a complete meal' (*Soncino Hebrew-English Ed., Bava Batra* 9a, note b(3). Moore states that 'one dried fig discharged obligations to him'

That the eminent[1] R. Papa was still of the opinion that the *baraita* still held suggests that the Sages dislike of the practice persisted well into the 4th Century CE. Despite the Tannaitic disdain for begging at doors, it may have been more widespread than they would like to admit, for example, a *baraita*[2] in *K'tubot* 67a stresses that a female orphan should take precedence over a male, מפני שהיא דרכו לחזור על הפתחים (because it is the way [i.e. not unusual] of a man to go about the doors [begging]) and also, in the *Mishnah*, an incident of the poor at the doorway is used as a case to deduce a Sabbath law, which suggests it was a common enough scenario and not necessarily always condemned.[3]

Indeed, begging at doorways may have become even more commonplace in the Amoraic period leading to R. Sama's very real concerns that if the Tannaitic view was still enforced this would be damaging. The view of the practice was apparently also changing, as highlighted in *Vayikra Rabbah* 34:9, which states,

א"ר אבין העני הזה עומד על פתחך והקב"ה עומד על ימינו דכתיב תהלים קט יעמוד לימין אביון אם נתת לו דע מי שעומד על ימינו ונותן לך שכרך ואם לא נתת לו דע מי שעומד על ימינו פורע ממך

...

(MOORE, *op. cit.*, p.117).

1. R. Papa was the main authority of his generation and founded a school at Naresh, near Sura. See STRACK & STEMBERGER, *op. cit.*, p.106.
2. In the *Sifre* anonymous teachings such as this are attributed by tradition ('since many of the passages offered [in *Sifre*] anonymously are in other Rabbinic texts presented in [his] name' (STRACK & STEMBERGER, *op. cit.*, p.296-7)) to R, Shim'on ben Yochai, a 3rd generation *Tanna* and student of R. Akiva to whose school the work is traditionally largely assigned.
3. *Shabbat* 1:1 speaks of העני עומד בחוץ ובעל הבית בפנים (the poor man standing outside and the master of the house [standing] within) and proceeds to explain which actions involved in carrying between private and public domains are permissible on *Shabbat* and which are not. The assumption in this Tannaitic source is that the householder is intending to give to the poor beggar at the door, even though this action would conflict with what we have learnt in our *Sifre* text.

(R. Abin[1] said, this poor man that stands at your door, the Holy One, Blessed be He stands at his right, as it is written, 'because he stands at the right hand of the needy' (*T'hillim* 109:31). If you give to him, know who it is that stands at his right [hand], and gives to you your reward, but if you do not give him, know who it is that stands at his right [hand], and will exact retribution from you ...).

This seems to indicate a dramatic change in the status of the needy person begging at the door, with a new tradition that God accompanies him. This in turn implies that the practice had become much more acceptable. Most likely this change in attitude reflected the fact that the practice was more commonplace and was a real problem that needed addressing in a more considerate manner than previously, It may also have been a reaction to a greater fear of punishment for not giving or perhaps a greater expectation of reward. For whatever reason, there was a reworking of the *halachah* to allow such a person to become a legitimate recipient of *ts'dakah*.[2]

Finally, on this subject, it is worth noting that we have so far interpreted this particular passage from *Sifre* fairly strictly. It should be noted that it uses the verb זקקין which mean 'to be legally obligated' or 'concerned',[3] and does not suggest you are forbidden to do so. Thus the *Tannaim* were not totally precluding giving voluntarily to such a person if one should wish to do so, only discouraging it.

In summary, whilst there are certain difficulties over the precise

---

1. Either R. Abin, the 4th generation *Amora* or his son, R. Abin II. Nevertheless this is a later development, around 300 CE.
2. From an historical perspective, it is also possible that the decline in Jewish autonomy led to a lessening of the role of the community funds which led to an increased acceptability of begging. There may also have been a reaction to the Christian charity ethic that would not have rejected doorway beggars which led to a relaxation of the *halachah* to ensure Judaism could not be accused of lower ethical standards.
3. JASTROW, *op. cit.*, p.410. Also 'to feel pain', 'to trouble oneself'.

reasons for some of the statements in this section of text, such as ולא באחרים and בכל מקום (in all places), the general thrust for the *Tannaim* is to utilise the Biblical text to shape practice or legitimise current norms regarding the priorities in giving *ts'dakah* amongst communities where the need would have been great and resources limited. Such priorities were to be determined by who was in the greatest of need, the relative closeness (by blood and by location) of the

poor person to the giver and the preference for adherence to the community's formal, structured methods of giving.

Section 2 - 'do not harden your heart'

לא תאמץ את לבבך יש בן אדם שמצער אם יתן אם לא יתן ולא
תקפוץ את ידך יש בן אדם שהוא פושט את ידו וחוזר וקופצה

('Do not harden your heart', there is one [kind of] person that agonises over whether he will give or not give. 'and do not close your hand' [and] there is [another kind of] person that stretches out his hand but [then] goes back [on the action] and closes it.)

The Rabbinical exegesis here exploits a parallelism in the Biblical text. One is expressly told not to do two things, either harden one's heart or close one's hand. The effect (i.e. not giving *ts'dakah*) is the same, therefore to avoid the accusation of redundancy in the text, each element must have been cited for a different reason. This reason, suggest the *Tannaim* of *Sifre*, is that the Biblical text is referring to two different kinds of person and two different circumstances.

Taking the two elements in order, we should note that the word לב is here, and indeed is usually, translated as 'heart'. This would imply to modern ears that the Biblical text is concerned primarily with the emotional aspect to the giving of *ts'dakah*, and that the warning לא תאמץ את לבבך is chiefly to one's feelings.[1]

However, in Rabbinical literature (and even more so in Biblical usage)

---

1. For example Hirsh explains of the verse that 'לא תאמץ את לבבך, literally: you shall not be strong against your heart ... assumes that Jewish hearts left to their natural bent are inclined to benevolence and this inclination can only be overcome by cold, calculating, selfish consideration' (HIRSCH, *op. cit.*, p.270).

the usual understanding of the word is 'mind'.¹ Moreover, the giving of *ts'dakah*, whilst undoubtedly a caring and considerate act, is nonetheless primarily conceived throughout Rabbinical literature as a rational and highly organised activity which is seen as providing the poor with that which is <u>rightfully theirs</u>.² The emotional element, whilst present is of lesser importance.

Though in Biblical usage the verb אמץ is often associated with strength, in Rabbinical understanding, it is 'to press' or 'harden',³ To 'be strong [against] one's heart' is therefore understood by the *Tannaim* as fixing ones mind in a certain course of action.⁴ Similar can be seen in the case of the Pharaoh of the Exodus, of whom it is said that God hardened his heart.⁵ This does not necessarily imply an emotional state but a mindset.

---

1. Jastrow renders '[innermost] heart, bosom; thought, inclination, mind' (JASTROW, op. cit., p.686).
2. 'Indeed to translate ... the Hebrew word *tzedakah* as "charity" (the usual translation) one misses the point that the Hebrew word comes from the root meaning Justice and righteousness: giving to the needy is a requirement, a matter of doing what is right. "Charity" comes from the Latin *caritas* - love or caring; the idea there is that the giving depends on the good will of the giver, not on the obligation to act with *tzedek* - justice.' (HOLTZ, op. cit., p.20-21). *Emek Han'tsiv* however, takes both meanings of the word to suggest some sort of contest between emotion and reason, explaining that,

    השכל מבין שיש לתן אבל לבבו חושב מחשבות און ומצטאר כי קשה אליו לגבר א' משתי אלה וע"ז בא הפסוק לא תאמץ את לבבך אלה תאמץ את שכלך

    ([his] reason understands that he should give but his heart thinks sinful thoughts and so he agonises, for it is difficult for him for either of these two to prevail, and because of this upon this the verse comes 'do not strengthen your heart' [against giving], rather strengthen your reason [to give]). He suggests that *Sifre*'s message is that you should not follow your emotions (לב) but your reason (שכל). This does seem a little unlikely, since for the *Tannaim*, לב was the seat of reason.
3. JASTROW, *op. cit.*, p.78.
4. Silbermann renders 'thou shalt not make thy heart obstinate'(SILBERMANN, *Pentateuch with Rashi's commentary: D'varim*, Jerusalem, 1934, p.80).
5. See *Sh'mot* Chapters 6-9, where this is given on numerous occasions.

The *Tannaim* explain that there are those who cannot make up their minds, one way or the other. Hence, these people are instructed not to[1] set their minds along the path of not giving.

מצטאר (agonise), is quite a strong word to employ and implies people who trouble themselves deeply or even feel anguish.[2] It may be that the *Tannaim* have in mind those people who worry that giving *ts'dakah* will actually impoverish them. Thus they are pained by the decision to give as much as being pained by the knowledge that not to give is a sin.

More difficult, however, is the exegesis on לא תקפוץ את ידך (do not close your hand). The intention to give is apparently affirmed in that the hand is stretched out, yet for some reason the action is not completed, חוזר (return) implying a change of mind.

Later in the *Sifre* text we learn of one who intends to give yet לא הספיק בידו (it is not sufficiently in his control [lit. hand]),[3] in that circumstances have changed in some way. It may be to such a one as this that the *Tannaim* are referring. However, in that case it is accepted that such a person is not at fault and still receives a reward for his intention to give, whilst one who closes his hand does not.

Toldot Adam suggests that in this instance the *Tannaim* are referring to a very specific case where one intends to give but the recipient has one *dinar*[4] less than the two hundred *zuzim*, which would classify him as a poor man. By giving him the *dinar* he would no longer be so classified

---

1. Montefiore/Loewe paraphrase, 'there are people who cause [themselves] pain whether they give or no. Be thou not so. harden not thy heart' (MONTEFIORE, C G, & LOEWE, H, *Charity,* from, *A Rabbinic Anthology*, MacMillan & Co., 1938, p.422.
2. JASTROW, *op. cit.*, p.1294. Silbermann renders the verb as 'painfully deliberate' (SILBERMANN, *op. cit.*, p.80).
3. Or possibly 'he does not have enough', *Sifre* to *D'varim* 15: 10. See section 12 for fuller discussion of this case and the various possible meanings of the *hiphil* form and see JASTROW, *op. cit.*, p.1016.
4. A small denomination silver coin, from the roman *dinardus,* also called a *zuz*.

and thus you might withhold it.¹ You are therefore warned, argues the commentator, not to close your hand, <u>even</u> in this particular circumstance.²

Whilst the explanations above may have some merit, it would seem that the *Sifre* text is somewhat more accusatory. It seems to imply a person who is willfully closing his hand after initially offering *ts'dakah*. It may be that the example brought by the *Tannaim* here is of a person for whom the intention to give was never really there at all, merely the appearance of it. Or perhaps someone who boasted that they gave a great deal but in reality gave relatively little.

By way of their illustration of these different types of people, the *Tannaim* have also introduced the idea of two stages in the giving of *ts'dakah*, the <u>intention</u> to give and the physical <u>act</u> itself. This will find an echo later in the *Sifre* text with separate rewards being promised for the voiced intention and the actual deed.³

Midrash Tannaim gives a *davar acher* (another interpretation), explaining,

ד"א לא תאמץ את לבבך מלדבר עליו ולא תקפוץ את ידך מליתן לו

('Do not harden your heart' from speaking about him to others 'and do not close your hand' from [actually] giving to him).⁴ Whilst not closing one's hand is here explained in a very straightforward manner, the first section of the verse is interpreted a little unexpectedly as a warning to alert others to the poor person's plight. Certainly we learn elsewhere⁵

---

1. *Toldot Adam* to לא תאמץ וכו'.
2. Since we are informed that,
    היו לא מאתים חסר דינר אפי' אלף נותנין לו כאחת הרי זה יטול (there was [a poor man] who had two hundred [*zuzim*] less one *dinar*, even if a thousand gave to him as one, he may take [the poor gifts] (*Pe'ah* 8:8), since 'if he has slipped below the poverty line, receipts from charity are not reckoned as changing his status' (MACCOBY, *op. cit.*, p.66).
3. See section 12 for discussion.
4. *Midrash Tannaim* to *D'varim* 15:7.
5. See section 12 for discussion.

that urging others to give leads to a reward, indeed a greater one than one's own giving, but the reason for the connection of this exegesis to לא תאמץ את לבבך (do not harden your heart) is not readily apparent.[1]

---

1. Elsewhere in *Midrash Tannaim* this idea is linked to the section on reward (*D'varim* 15:10)
   ד"א כי בגלל הדבר הזה יב' ה' אלהיך בגלל שדברת עליו לאחרים וה"א והיה מעשה הצדקה שלום
   (another interpretation 'for because of this thing the Lord your God will bless you', because you spoke about him to others, as it says [in *Y'shayah* 32:17] 'and the causers of righteousness [understood as charity] will have peace').

Section 3 - 'your end will be to take from him'

מאחיך האביון אם אין אתה לו סופך ליטול הימנו

('From your brother, the needy person'. If you do not give to him your end [will be] to take from him.)

Whilst later our *midrash* will spend much time discussing the rewards of giving, and the punishments for not doing so, the first mention of punishment is relatively terse. Here, the *Tannaim* appear to be concerned to explain a superfluous repetition of אחיך (your brother).[1] We have already had mention of the needy being 'your brother' and this has been explained as implying an hierarchy in giving.[2] If one accepts that no word in *Torah* is redundant,[3] then for the Rabbis this second usage must carry some other meaning. Their suggestion is that it should be read as a metaphor for the closeness between oneself and the needy, in that were you to close your heart and your hand, then, as Rashi, paraphrasing the *Sifre* text, would have us understand the verse, אם לו תתן לו סופך להיות אחיו של אביון (if you do not give to him,

---

1. סופך ליטול הימנו דמאחיך מיותר ודריש דסופו להיות אחיו ורגיל עמו ('and your end will be to take from him' - [derived] from the superfluous 'from your brother', that his end will be to be his [i.e. the poor's] brother and regularly be with him) (*Emek Han'tsiv*). This idea is not conveyed well by Hammer's rendering 'from thy needy brother' (HAMMER, *op. cit.*, p.161) rather than 'from your brother, the needy person'.
2. See section 1.
3. In Rabbinical literature this is a given, since 'the Torah's being is treated as a kind of figurative extension of God's [attributes] ... just as all His deeds are meaningful, so every word in the Torah is full of significance' (STERN, D, *Midrash*, from COHEN & MENDES-FLOHR, *op. cit.*, p.619).

[then] your end is to be the brother of the poor).[1]

This idea of a punishment which balances the sin is well established in Scripture and in Rabbinical literature and is part of a system of justice which works on the principle of *middah k'neged middah* (measure for measure),[2] for example,

תניא ר' מאיר אומר במדה שאדם מודד מודדין לו דכתיב בסאסאה בשלחה תריבנה

(it has been taught, R. Meir[3] says, in the measure which a man measures, will it be measured [out] to him, as it is written, 'in measure when it shoots forth, you will contend with it'. (*Y'shayah* 27:8)).[4]

However, whilst in the *Sifre* text, the idea of such a punishment is linked homiletically to מאחיך האביון, elsewhere in Rabbinical Literature this idea is developed with reference to other verses from *D'varim* 15:7-11. Though this will represent a departure from our core analysis of the *Sifre* text, it is worth exploring this concept further through these texts, in order to understand more fully the views the *Tannaim* (and later the *Amoraim*) held with regard to the reciprocal nature of sin and punishment for not giving *ts'dakah*.

---

1. Rashi to *D'varim* 15:7.
2. 'Numerous dicta, aphorisms, stories and parables were added by the Sages to those already in the Bible in order to prove that the principle 'measure for measure' was not abolished' (URBACH, *op. cit.*, p.439).
3. R. Meir, 3rd Generation *Tanna*, see STRACK & STEMBERGER, op. cit., p.84.
4. *Sanhedrin* 100a. 'i.e. in the same measure that sin spreads, so it is punished, and conversely, the same holds good of righteousness - the conception of 'measure for measure' (Soncino Hebrew-English Ed., note d(3). For Biblical examples, see *Sh'mot* 21:24-25,

    עין תחת עין שן תחת שן יד תחת יד רגל תחת רגל כויה תחת כויה פצע תחת פצע חבורה תחת חבורה

    (eye for an eye, tooth for tooth, hand for hand, foot for foot, burning for burning, wound for wound, bruise for bruise). Also see *Iyyov* 34:11,

    כי פעל אדם ישלם לו וכארח איש ימצאנו (for according to the work of a man, He will requite him, and according to his ways will He make it befall him).

For the Sages quoted in *Midrash Tannaim* their point of departure is instead *D'varim* 15:8, where the idea forms part of a lengthy section commenting on פתח תפתח ('you will surely open'),

ד"א פתח תפתח היה ר' יונתן בן יוסף אומר הנתן מתוך הדוחק סופו ליתן מתוך העושר והחושך מתוך העושר סופו לחשוך מתוך הדוחק

(another interpretation [on] ''for you will surely open'. R. Yonatan ben Yosef[1] was wont to say, one who gave from the midst of need, his end will be to give from the midst of riches, and one who holds back from [giving] when he is in the midst of riches, his end will be to hold back from the midst of need).[2]

As well as the parallel to the *Sifre* text that one who witholds *ts'dakah* will end up needing to benefit from it, the reverse of the coin is also presented.[3] This text also moves the argument a step further, to explain that this is not mere chance, but that God will <u>engineer</u> it,

אמר רבי כל מי שהוא עושה צדקה מעוני הקב"ה מכפיל לו פרנסתו ואינו מחסרו דכת' נותן לרש אין מחסור אבל מי שיש לו ממון ומעלים עיניו הקב"ה נותן מארה באותו הממון דכת' ומעלים עיניו רב מארות

(Rabbi[4] said all who perform *ts'dakah* from [a state of] poverty, the Holy One, Blessed be He, doubles for him his livelihood, and He causes him not to lack [anything], as it is written 'he [who] gives to the poor shall not lack' (*Mishley* 28.27). But he who has wealth and hides

---

1. 2nd generation *Tanna*.
2. *Midrash Tannaim* to *D'varim* 15:8.
3. Similarly, *Y'rushalmi Pe'ah* 8: 8 states,

   וכל מי שאינו צריך ליטול ונוטל אינו מת מן הזקנה עד שיצטך לבריות וכל מי שהוא צריך ליטול ואינו נוטל אינו מת מן הזקנה עד שיפרנס לאחרים

   (and whoever does not need to take but takes [from charity funds] will not die from old age until he is dependent [lit. joined to] on [other] people and whoever needs to take and do not take, will not die from old age until he supports others).
4. *Y'hudah Hanasi*, 6th generation *Tanna*, known simply as רבי, (Rabbi, *par excellence*), the redactor of the *Mishnah*.

his eyes[1] [from the poor], the Holy One, blessed be He places a curse on that same wealth, as it says 'he who hides his eyes [shall have] many a curse').[2]

In most other texts, however, the verse taken as the base for demonstrating this concept of reciprocal punishment is *D'varim* 15:10, which in its context actually describes the reward attendant on performing the *mitsvah*.

The primary text for this development appears to be *Shabbat* 151b where it is reported that,

תניה ר' אליעזר הקפר אומר לעולם יבקש אדם רחמים על מדה זו שאם לא בא בא בנו ואם בנו לא בן בנו שנאמר כי בגלל הדבר הזה

(it was taught [that] R. Eliezer Hakappar[3] said, a person [should] always seek mercy concerning this measure [of punishment for not giving charity], for if it does not come [to him], it will come to his son, and if not to his son, it will come to his son's son, as it is said 'for because of this thing').

How this exegesis has been formed is explained by one of the school of R. Yishma'el,[4] תני דבי ר' ישמעאל שגלגל הוא שחוזר בעולם (it was taught by one of the School of R. Yishma'el that it is a wheel that turns in the world). By use of creative philology,[5] the Sages have reinterpreted בגלל (because of) as גלגל (a wheel) and have thereby given a name to the concept of balanced retribution with regard to *ts'dakah* provision.

---

1. See section 9 on ורעה עינך (and your eye be evil).
2. *Midrash Tannaim* to *D'varim* 15:8.
3. R. Eliezer Hakappar, 4th generation *Tanna*, see STRACK & STEMBERGER, *op. cit.*, p.88.
4. Yishmael ben Elisha, 2nd generation *Tanna*. *Ibid.*, p.79
5. 'Puns and word plays, reversals of letters and convergence of sounds' (HOLTZ, *op. cit.*, p.189).

Moore suggests that this reasoning has been 'sparked off' by the use of בגלל instead of the more common למען [therefore][1] and it seems that whilst the authors of *Sifre* were content to interpret *D'varim* 15:10 in light of rewards, expanding only on the content of the verse, the school of R. Yishma'el held a separate tradition that the verse also represented a statement of punishment. This, in itself, is interesting as it is has traditionally been thought that the school of R. Yishma'el take the more literal rendering and try to avoid such linguistic play.[2]

It is also worthy of note that instead of suggesting that סופך ליטול הימנו (your end [will be] to take from him), the punishment can now cross generations and be visited on בנו (his [i.e. the sinner's] son) or בן בנו (his grandson). Perhaps the later Sages had witnessed, more often than not, that the promised retribution did not necessarily come to sinners in their own lifetimes and indeed that those who acted righteously still suffered.[3] In order to try to protect the idea that God did mete out balanced retribution, from a reality that did not reflect this, the extension was posited.[4]

---

1. MOORE, *op. cit.*, p.169.
2. Typically, 'R. Ishmael [and his school] approached the text by the use of highly formalized and technical methods of interpretation and did not assume that the interpretations could be based on peculiarities of language ("Scripture uses normal language")' (HAMMER, *op. cit.*, p.8).
3. 'The conventional 'doctrine of reward and punishment' underwent a grave crisis in the period of Hadrian's religious persecution, which led to a change in Rabbinic thinking on theodicy [since] resolve to observe the commandments was itself the cause of death and suffering' (URBACH, *op. cit.*, p.442). Cohen notes that 'the people were perplexed over the triumph of the Godless Romans [and that] not without cause did a Rabbi utter the exhortation: 'Abandon not belief in retribution (*Aboth* 1:7)'' (COHEN, A, *Everyman's Talmud*, Schocken Books, Random House Inc., New York, 1988, p.114).
4. Elsewhere in Rabbinical literature there is much discussion over Scriptural passages that suggest the sins of the father can be visited upon succeeding generations. The general conclusion was that this is only if the succeeding generations continue to hate God and sin against Him. Rewards too can span generations, for example *Midrash Tannaim* to *D'varim* 15:8 teaches that,

    וכל מי שהוא נותן צדקה לפועלי תורה הקב"ה שומרו לאלף דור (and he that

Certainly in the case already referred to concerning R. Chiyya, the concern is not for his own reward or punishment rather,

אמר לה ר' חייא לדביתהו כי אתי עניא אקדימי ליה ריפתא כי היכי דלקדמו לבניך

(R. Chiyya said to her [his wife] if a poor [person] comes, be quick to [give to) to him bread, so that [others will] be quick [to give] to your children).[1]

This fear for the well-being of one's children, as opposed to oneself, is confirmed by the *Tannaim* in *Rosh Hashana* 4a, which states,

והתניא אומר סלע זו לצדקה בשביל שיחיו בני ובשביל שאזכה לחיי העולם הבא הרי זה צדיק גומר

(it was taught [in a *baraita*] one who says this *sela* is for charity so that my son shall live, or that I merit life in the world to come, behold, he is wholly righteous). Urbach argues that 'this *baraita* reflects a widespread belief amongst the people [about reward and punishment] which the Sages continued to strengthen and even utilise in urging the observance of commandment'.[2]

The key element, which saw later development by the Rabbis, was the גלגל (wheel) and the image that is conjured up by later texts is that of the wheel turning. The overall impression presented is very fatalistic, in that only God makes rich and poor and He alone[3] can decide which a

---

gives *t'sdakah* to scholars [lit. workers of the Law], The Holy One, Blessed be He guards him unto a thousand generations).

1. *Shabbat* 151b.
2. URBACH, *op. cit.*, p.436.
3. As *Midrash Tannaim* to *D'varim* 15:8 explains,

ואם אינו נותן לו עליהם הכ' אומר עשיר ורש נפגשו עשה כולם ה' מי שעשה לזה עשיר יכול לעשתו עני ומי שעשה לזה עני יכול לעשתו עשיר

(and if he does not give to him, about such a one Scripture says 'The poor and the rich meet together, the Lord makes [them] all' (*Mishley* 22:2). He who makes this one rich is able to make him poor and He who makes this one poor will be able to make him rich. Similarly Ben Sira explains, 'good fortune and bad, life and death, poverty and wealth all come from the Lord' (*Ecclesiasticus (The Wisdom of Ben*

person will be. The image is enhanced in *Vayikra Rabbah* 34:9,

א"ר נחמן כי בגלל הדבר הזה אהן עלמא מדמי לגלגלא דאנטילא דמלא מתרוקן דמתרוקן מתמלא

(R. Nachman[1] said, 'for because of this thing', [implies] this world is a water-wheel (*galgela*), through which the full is emptied and the empty filled). In this metaphor, the 'full' are the rich and the 'empty' are the poor.

Finally, in what seems like coming full circle, *Sh'mot Rabbah*,[2] gives an interpretation to את העני עמך (the poor <u>with you</u>),[3] a phrase which is itself reminiscent of the 'closeness' implied by מאחיך האביון (<u>your</u> brother, the needy person)[4] and which therefore receives a similar treatment,

ד"א את העני עמך הה"ד כי האלהים שופט זה ישפיל וזה ירים למה דומה העולם הזה לגלגל שבגנה כלי חרס שבו התחתונים עולים מלאים והעליונים יורדין ריקנין כך לא כל מי שהוא עשיר היום הוא עשיר למחר ולא מי שהוא עני היום עני למחר למה שגלגל הוא בעולם כי בגלל הדבר הזה

(another interpretation [of], 'the poor with you'. Scripture says elsewhere 'for God is judge. One [person] He will cast down [and] one [person] He will raise up'. To what is this world to be compared? To a wheel that is in a garden, [the] earthen vessels at the bottom come up full and those at the top descend empty. Thus not all who are rich today will be rich tomorrow and not all who are poor today will be poor tomorrow. Why? Because the world is a wheel (*galgal*), [as it says] for

---

Sira) 11:14, *The New English Bible: The Apocrypha*, Oxford and Cambridge University Press, 1970, p.176.
1. R. Nachman bar Ya'akov, 3rd generation Babylonian *Amora*, see STRACK & STEMBERGER, op. cit., p.101.
2. A much later Midrashic work, probably edited after the 16th Century but which does draw on earlier Tannaitic Literature.
3. *Sh'mot* 22:24.
4. Rashi to *Sh'mot* 22:24 gives, את העני עמך הוי מסתכל בעצמו כאילו אתה עני ('the poor with you' - regard yourself as if you are the poor person).

'because of (*biglal*) this thing ...').[1]

In our discussion of the development of the concept of *galgal*, we have moved quite far away from the *Sifre* text, and the period to which it belongs. Nonetheless, it is clear that the short sentence in *Sifre* supports the continued belief of the *Tannaim* in a measured retribution and that the Biblical idea of *'middah k'neged middah'* was quite applicable to the case of withholding *ts'dakah*. Moreover, whichever text the concept was applied to as time progressed, the message is essentially the same; that if you do not give *ts'dakah*, your punishment will be to be a 'brother' to the poor, in that you or your descendents will become one of their number.[2]

---

1. *Sh'mot Rabbah* 31:14.
2. An interesting lesson for us today in that how often we hear people propose a seemingly selfish reason to, for example, give blood or become an organ donor or donate to a specific cause like Cancer Research: 'You never know, one day you or your family will need this and benefit from it.'

Section 4 - 'even a hundred times'

שאם פתחת פעם אחת אתה פותח אפילו מאה פעמים תלמוד לומר
כי פתוח תפתח את ידך לו

(From where [do we learn that) if you [have] opened once, you [should] open even a hundred times, Scripture says 'you will surely open [lit. opening, you will open] to him').

Throughout the *Sifre* passage, and indeed throughout Rabbinic literature we see a continuing concern to explain the wide use of the Infinitive Absolute[1] in Scripture.

'All the commandments of benevolence are here proclaimed in amplifying form פתח תפתח, נתון תתן, העבט תעביטנו',[2] and whilst from a grammatical viewpoint this is generally understood as being a device that 'expresses emphasis'[3] - for many of the early Rabbis, the use of the form instead signifies either a repetition or an extension to the duty, or even both.[4]

---

1. The Infinitive Absolute is used to add emphasis or certainty to the verb. This usage is commonplace in the Bible. Weingreen explains that 'it expresses emphasis when it immediately precedes the finite verb, and duration when it immediately follows it' and 'is sometimes used to represent the Imperative' (WEINGREEN, J, *A Practical Grammar for Classical Hebrew, 2nd Ed.*, Clarenden Press, Oxford, 1959, p.79).
2. HIRSCH, *op, cit.*, p.270.
3. WEINGREEN, *op. cit.*, p.79.
4. Hirsch suggests that 'the unlimited times one has to repeat ones charity actions - even a hundred times - lies already in the indefinite tense of the infinitive ... whilst the addition of the definite tense extends the duty also in other directions' (HIRSCH, *op. cit.*, p.270).

Here in *Sifre*, we have what appears to be a standard interpretative form which will be used later in our passage to comment on נתון תתן (you will surely give),[1] and is used again shortly after that, in the case of the emancipated slave.[2]

It is unlikely that there is any significance in the use of 'one hundred times',[3] other than that it represents a large number and as such suits the exaggerative stance of the exegesis.[4] It is brought simply to emphasise the need to ensure a <u>continual flow</u> of *ts'dakah*.

Elsewhere in Rabbinic literature, though, the use of the infinitive absolute in *D'varim* 15:7-11 is given other meanings. A fine example of this is to be found in *baraitot* presented in *Bava M'tsia* 31b where all

---

1. מנין אם נתת פעם אחת תן לו אפילו מאה פעמים תלמוד לומר נתון תתן
(From where [do we learn that] if you gave to him once, you give to him even a hundred times, Scripture says 'you will surely give' (*Piska* 117 on *D'varim* 15:10).
2. מנין שאם הענקת פעם אחת הענק לו אפילו מאה פעמים תלמוד לומר הענק תעניק
(From where [do we learn] that if you furnished him [with gifts] once you will furnish him even a hundred times Scripture says 'you will surely grant' (*Piska* 119 on *D'varim* 15:14).
3. Though *Toldot Adam* does suggest that it relates to שער הברכה (the gates of blessing) which in turn are connected to *B'reshit* 26:12,
ויזרע יצחק בארץ ההוא וימצא בשנה ההוא מאה שערים (and Yitschak sowed in that place and found in it [i.e. received from it] <u>one hundred fold</u> [lit. gates]).
4. Certainly by Amoraic times this appeared to be a standard interpretation which denied the idea that infinitive absolute meant only twice. For example in *Bava M'tsia* 31a we read that of returning property,
אמר ליה ההוא מדרבנן לרבא אימא השב חדא זמנא תשיבם תרי זמני אמר ליה השב אפילו מאה פעמים משמע
(one of the Rabbis said to Rava, perhaps 'restore' implies once and 'you will restore' implies twice. He [Rava] said to him 'restore' even one hundred times). Similar treatment is also given to (you will תשלח surely let go [the dam] (*D'varim* 22:6,7)) and to הוכח תוכיח (you will surely rebuke [your neighbour] (*Vayikra* 19: 17)) also in *Bava M'tsia* 31a.

the uses in these verses are commented on in quick succession,[1]

פתח תפתח אין לי אלא לעניי עירך לעניי עיר אחרת מנין תלמוד לומר פתח תפתח מכל מקום נתן תתן אין לי אלא מתנה מרובה מתנה מועטת מנין תלמוד לומר נתן תתן מכל מקום

('you will surely open', I only know this of the poor of your own city, from where [do I learn it also applies] to the poor of another city, Scripture says 'you will surely open' [implying] in all cases. 'You will surely give', I only know this of a large gift, from where [do I learn it also applies] to a small gift, Scripture says 'you will surely give').

It is likely that our *Sifre* text does not utilise פתח תפתח to present the idea of giving to other cities since this is already implied by its earlier statement that יושבי עירך קודמים ליושבי עיר אחרת ([the] inhabitants of your city before [the] inhabitants of another city).[2]

The comment that *Bava M'tsia* 31b attaches to נתון תתן (you will surely give) does present a new idea worth exploration. It introduces a case where אי אפשר לך ליתן מתנה מרובה (it is impossible for you to give a large gift),[3] and concludes that nonetheless you are still obliged to give *ts'dakah*. The Sages utilise the infinitive absolute to extend the duty so that 'it is not confined to rich people who can give big amounts but also to less rich people from whom the fulfilment of the duty is equally expected even if they can only give the very smallest amount'.[4]

---

1. Including העבט תעביטנו (you will surely loan) which *Sifre* makes no comment on, with regard to the verb structure. This phrase is discussed in section 5. Near identical expositions to those of *Bava M'tsia* 31b, are also to be found in *Midrash Tannaim* as comments on these same sections.
2. *Piska* 116 to *D'varim* 15:7. 'Here עניי עיר אחרת is learnt from the רבוי פתח תפתח whereas according to the Sifri, this is already expressed by עניי עירך in בשעריך as well as those בארצך' (HIRSCH, *op. cit.*, p.271).
3. Rashi to *Bava M'tsia* 31b, מתנה מועטת מנין (a small gift, from where [do we learn this]).
4. HIRSCH, *op. cit.*, p.270.

This statement may even be implying an extension of the duty to those who would normally be recipients of *ts'dakah* themselves, for according to *Tosefta Pe'ah* 4:10, עני שנתן פרוטה לקופה ופרוסה לתמחוי מקבלין אותו ממנו (a poor man who gave a *p'rutah*[1] to the *kuppah*[2] or a piece of bread to the *tamchui*[3] we receive them from him).[4]

From the references above, we can see that the *Tannaim* appear to have held that ideally <u>everyone</u> (even the needy), should give *ts'dakah* and also on <u>numerous occasions</u>, whenever the opportunity presented itself.

That said, it is important to note, however, that not all the *Tannaim* agreed that the use of the infinitive absolute in Scripture was indicative of either a repetition or an extension of the duty. Rather, some argued that דברה תורה כלשון בני אדם (the Torah speaks in the language of man); i.e. the *Torah* 'employs human phraseology'[5] and thus no

---

1. 'The smallest copper coin', MACCOBY, *op. cit.*, p.135, a minimum amount.
2. 'Literally 'basket'. This was the substantial communal fund for giving a whole week's sustenance to the poor, a distribution being made every Friday' (*ibid.*, p.65-66).
3. 'The charity plate ... derived from *michyah* ('provision'). This was a collection plate from which were provided daily distributions of food for the poor' (*ibid.*, p.65).
4. 'The obligation to give charity is incumbent on the poor too' (*ibid.*, p.135, though the *Tosefta* text does add that, אם לא נתן אין מחייבין אותו ליתן (if he doesn't give we do not bind him to give). Certainly, by late Amoraic times, it was definitely expected that the poor would contribute, אמר מר זוטרא אפי' עני המתפרנס מן הצדקה יעשה צדקה (Mar Zutra 15th generation Babylonian *Amora* said, even a poor person who is supported from *ts'dakah* [should] give [lit. do] *ts'dakah*) (*Gittin* 7b).
5. *Bava M'tsia* 31b, Soncino Hebrew-English Ed., translation.

particular conclusion could be drawn from the use of such a grammatical form.[1]

---

1. For example R. Shim'on b. Yochai (3rd generation *Tanna*) and R. Eleazar b. Azariah (3rd generation *Tanna*) who both use the phrase in dismissing other exegeses on העבט תעביטנו (you will surely lend) and הענק תעניק (you will surely furnish [the emancipated slave with gifts]) respectively in *Bava M'tsia* 31b. The principle is attributed to R. Yishmael in *K'ritot* 11a, who 'was known to prefer a plain method of interpretation as a rule' (MACCOBY, *op. cit.*, p.161). See section 5 for further discussion of this principle.

Section 5 - 'to embolden his spirit'

> והעבט תעביטנו פתוח תפתח פתח לו בדברים שאם היה ביישן אמור
> לו את צריך ללוות מיכן אמרו צדקה ניתנת כמלווה
> והעבט תעביטנו נותנים לו וחוזרים וממשכנים אותו דברי ר' יהודה
> וחכמים אומ' אומרים לו הבא משכון כדי להגיס דעתו

('And you will surely lend him', 'you will surely open', open [the conversation] for him with words, that if he was ashamed, say to him, "Do you need to borrow?" From this they said, *ts'dakah* [should be] given as a loan. 'You will surely lend to him', we give to him and [then] return and take from him a pledge, these are the words of Rabbi Y'hudah, but the Sages say, we say to him "Bring a pledge!", in order to embolden his spirit).

The idea of lending charity may appear odd, even if the loan is interest free.[1] However, as worthwhile as giving charity is, in the end it is self defeating; perpetuating the very existence that it is trying to eradicate by creating a dependent class who rely upon the 'hand-outs' of the

---

1. The Torah commands that,

    אם־כסף תלוה את־עמי את־העני עמך לא־תהיה לו כנשה לא־תשימון עליו נשך

    (if you lend money to My people, to the poor among you, you are not to act as a creditor to him; you shall not charge him interest. (*Sh'mot* 22:24)) as well as the Biblical injunction,

    את־כספך לא־תתן לו בנשך ובמרבית לא־תתן אכלך (you shall not give him your money for interest, nor may you give him your food for increase (*Vayikra* 25:37)).

more fortunate.[1] The Biblical text itself is concerned with lending and specifically the need to carry on this lending when the seventh year approached. Also, as *Ben Sira* explains, a 'devout man lends to his neighbour, by supporting him he keeps the commandments' and enjoins us to 'lend to [our] neighbour at his time of need'.[2]

However, 'the [Biblical] laws ... contemplate a population living in simple conditions, chiefly on the land'[3] and 'it is evident from our sources that the provision for the poor contemplated by the Law, even with a liberal interpretation was inadequate under the actual conditions and that other measures were necessary'.[4]

To this end, the Sages appear to be trying to 'hijack' this section of *Torah* and widen its application by making it apply primarily to general gifts of *ts'dakah*. Such a stance would have been more applicable in their own times where the elaborate communal funds were largely given as gifts rather than as loans.

Wishing to concentrate on gifts, their immediate problem is why Scripture should state categorically that one should lend to a person, as well as saying 'open' and 'give', which are more suggestive of gifts. In

---

1. For example Maimonides states that the,
מעלה גדולה שאין למעלה ממנה זה המחזיק ביד ישראל שמך ונותן לו מתנה או הלואה או עושה עמו שותפות או ממציא לו מלאכה כדי לחזק את ידו עד שלא יצטרך לבריות (the highest level [of *ts'dakah*, which has no [level] higher than it - this is the strengthening of the hand of the Israelite who become poor, and giving him a gift or a loan or making a partnership with him or finding him work so that his hand is strengthened until he no longer need ask [anything] of any one (*Mishneh Torah: Hilchot Mat'not Aniyim* 10:7)). By strengthening his hand, the Rambam means bringing the poor person to a means whereby he may become self supporting. He draws this argument from *Vayikra* 25:35 which reads,
והחזקת בו גר ותושב וחי עמך (and you shall strengthen [support] him, the stranger or the settler and he will live with you). See Appendix 1.
2. *Eccleslasticus* 29:1-2, *op. cit.*, p.207.
3. MOORE, *op. cit.*, p.162.
4. *Ibid.*, p.163.

response to this they build an elaborate construction to ensure the terms are not in conflict but are compatible; suggesting that Scripture intended that צדקה ניתנת כמלוה (*ts'dakah* [should be] given as a loan). Our first question is then whether by this the *Tannaim* meant merely 'in the appearance of' or whether this was a <u>real</u> loan of sorts that would eventually be collected upon.

The initial section, in the Finkelstein text, appears only in two versions,[1] but whilst it may not have been part of the original text, it does, nonetheless, fit the overall theme of the section well. The suggestion is that one should understand העבט תעביטנו (you will surely lend) in light of the words פתוח תפתח (you will surely open),[2] but whereas in Scripture[3] this was intended very much as a physical opening of יד (your hand), it is used here in a sense that is familiar in Rabbinic terminology, namely to open a conversation or discourse.[4] One is instructed to speak to the poor person first, but only, apparently אם היה ביישן (if he was ashamed). ביישן could also be read as 'timid' or 'bashful',[5] in that perhaps he does not wish to come forward. In *Midrash Tannaim*, however, we find,

ד״א כי פתח תפתח ר׳ ישמעאל אומר אם היה בן טובים ובוש ואומר בדברים ואומר לו בני שמא צריך ללוות מיכן אמרו צדקה ניתנת כמלוה

---

1. In פ and ר, i.e. 97 פירוש ר׳ הלל כת״י בפראנקפורט מערצבאכער and כת״י רומי של כל הספרי (FINKELSTEIN, *op. cit.*, p.175).
2. Though arguably this is solely an exegesis on פתוח תפתח that is out of place - see *Midrash Tannaim* 15:8.
3. And indeed in *Sifre* itself, See section 2.
4. For example, of the son who is unable to ask at the Seder table, one is told את פתח לו (you open [the conversation] for him). The use of פתח implying opening a discourse can be seen employed particularly in the Midrashic *P'tichah* (or Proem), a form employed freely in works such as *B'reshit Rabbah* and *Vayikra Rabbah*, see STRACK & STEMBERGER, *op. cit.*, p.267ff.
5. JASTROW, *op. cit.*, p. 181.

(another interpretation on 'for you will surely open'. R. Yishmael says, if he was of good family[1] and ashamed we engage him with words and say, "My son, perhaps you need to borrow?" From this they said *ts'dakah* [should be) given as a loan).[2]

Given that one would not necessarily know whether the person was ashamed until they offered some resistance to a gift, unless they were readily identifiable as a בן טובים ([poor person] of good family), it is possible that the *Sifre* teaching appears more fully formed in *Midrash Tannaim*.[3] Here also this case appears restricted only to an occasion for when one does know the circumstances of this person, who was previously well off, yet has fallen on hard times and would therefore be more likely to react badly to a gift.[4]

If this was the case, then the words that one opens with would be those which follow in the text, i.e. את צריך ללות (Do you need to borrow?)[5] However, if one does not know whether the person would be ashamed, then arguably one might need to engage the poor person in

---

1. See sections 6 and 12 for discussion of the עני בן טובים.
2. *Midrash Tannaim* to *D'varim* 15:8.
3. The citation of a named *Tanna* may be a further support to this.
4. That said there may be other signs of a poor person being embarrassed to take, such as his body language, in that they he be hanging back or looking uneasy even before the original approach is made. In which case timid or bashful may be acceptable translations of the *Sifre* version.
5. Lieberman to *Tosefta Pe'ah* 4: 12 states,

פותחים לו בדברים ואומרים לו ובשביל ששמענו שנפלה לך ירושה ממקום אחר טול ואתה פורע

(And we open to him with words and say to him, because we have heard that an inheritance has fallen to you from a different place, take [now] and pay us back [later] (LIEBERMAN, S, *Tosefta Ki-Fshutah: A Comprehensive Commentary on the Tosefta (8 vols), Pe'ah*, New York, 1955-73, p.187)). However, drawing on *Y'rushalmi Peah* 8:9 and *Vayikrah Rabbah* 34:1, it is quite clear that having told the poor person to pay them back later,

בשעה שנותנו לו היה אומר לו מתנה לך נתתיו (at the time that he was given [the 'loan'] he was wont to say to him, [it is] a gift I have given to you).

conversation to assess that person's needs and to find out their personal circumstances.

It may be that where the *Sifre* text differs from *Midrash Tannaim*, by not identifying the person immediately as a בן טובים, there is a suggestion that פתח לו בדברים (open to him with words) implies instead a short preliminary conversation, which is offered to assess the circumstances first.

Only <u>after</u> it is determined that the person would be embarrassed, for whatever reason,[1] do they offer the *ts'dakah* as a loan.

Regardless of whether this case is restricted to only the בן טובים or whether it applies to any one who might be similarly embarrassed, the Rabbinic notion of *bushah* (shame) is paramount here.[2] Indeed, this concept is to be found as an underlying theme throughout our *Sifre* text, and hence the translation of בייש as 'ashamed' is preferred.

Finally, our reading of the case above also affects our understanding of the phrase that follows, מיכן אמרו צדקה ניתנת כמלוה (from this they said *ts'dakah* [should be] given as a loan), מיכן (from this) suggests that it is this case that specifically led to the statement by the

---

1. Not necessarily only concerning his previous status, as there may be other reasons for his embarrassment.
2. This notion is illustrated in Rabbinic literature by such extreme statements as,

ואמר רב זוטרא בר טוביה אמר רב, ואמרי לה אמר רב חנא בר ביזנא אמר רבי שמעון חסידא, ואמרי לה אמר רבי יוחנן משום רבי שמעון בן יוחי נוח לו לאדם שיפיל עצמו לתוך כבשן האש ואל ילבין פני חברו ברבים

(R. Zutra b. Tuvyah said [in the name of] Rav, [or] others say, R. Channa b. Biznah said [in the name of] R. Shim'on the pious, [or] others say, R. Yochanan said [in the name of] R. Shim'on b. Yochai, better for a man that he should cast himself into a fiery furnace than to shame [lit. whiten the face of] his fellow in public (*B'rachot* 43b)). With so many rabbis laying possible claim to this statement, it must have been a very widely held view! See *K'tubot* 67b and *Sota* 10b for other examples.

Sages.[1] Does this imply that the statement is similarly restricted to the case where the person would be embarrassed, or, is the statement a widening by the Rabbis suggesting that *ts'dakah* should be given as a loan in all instances?

The answers perhaps lie in the second section of the *Sifre* text and the parallels to this. However, it is this latter section of the text where there seems to be the most disagreement, both from scholars about how the text should actually read and also from the Sages themselves, as regards what is the proper course of action when meeting a poor man.

Taking the *Sifre* text at face value, R. Y'hudah's[2] opinion is that, נותנים לו וחוזרים וממשכנים אותו (we give to him and [then] return to take a pledge[3] [from] him. This alone presents a conflict within the *Sifre* text since from the initial passage discussed above, we could infer that the initial approach is to present it as a loan and not as a gift. It may be that R. Y'hudah is speaking of one whom we knew would not be embarrassed by a gift, or perhaps this is his view of the order of presentation regardless of the poor person's circumstances or feelings.

It would appear, though, that his view is a minority opinion since the text states והחמים אומרים (but [lit. 'and' though this is usually taken to imply a disagreement] the Sages say). The Sages comment that we take a pledge כדי להגיס את דעתו (in order to embolden his spirit), i.e. to make him feel better about the whole transaction appears to correspond with the opening passage in this section and also implies

---

1. 'L. Ginsberg has pointed out ... that there are many places in Tannaitic *Midrashim* in which this phrase (*mik-kan 'omru*) may refer to a collection of Midrashic laws which were older than the *Mishnah* and from which the *Mishnah* itself drew its formulations' (HAMMER, *op. cit.*, p. 388, note 19). If so, these ideas could be very early indeed.
2. R. Y'hudah b. Ilai, 3rd generation *Tanna*. See STRACK & STEMBERGER, *op, cit.*, p.84.
3. משכון (a pledge, security (JASTROW, *op. cit.*, p. 854)) could be seized by the creditor if the loan was not repaid.

that it is given first as a loan and then as a gift, but again it is not stated explicitly.

Though it seems unlikely, one could argue that the Sages statement could apply equally alongside that of R. Y'hudah's, as it only relates to the reason for the pledge itself and not <u>when</u> it is taken.[1] Moreover, in other sources, as we shall see, the Sages opinion can be that it is presented initially as a gift.

Thus, aside from the questions already raised above, we are now unsure of where the *Tannaim* stand as regards the order of presentation. Is it a loan which is then announced to be a gift, or a gift which becomes a loan?

Fortunately, similar discussions of how *ts'dakah* should be offered take place in a number of other sources, notably *Tosefta Pe'ah* 4:12-13, *K'tubot* 67b (where there are two versions) and *Bava M'tsia* 31b and these help our understanding of the *Sifre* passage.

Unlike *Sifre*, these texts all make the distinction between one who cannot support himself and yet does not want to take charity - presumably from pride[2] - and one who can afford to support himself but doesn't wish to - presumably out of greed or laziness.

---

1. I.e. reading ו literally as 'and', so that the phrase read 'we give to him and [then] return and take from him a pledge, these are the words of R. Y'hudah, and the Sages [who agree with this order] say, we say to him [when we return to him] "Bring a pledge!" in order to embolden his spirits'. Both Neusner and Hammer appear to have perceived a difficulty here and avoid it by not translating ו, thus they do not link the two statements in any way, (NEUSNER, *op. cit.*, p.290 and HAMMER, *op. cit.*, p.162 respectively).
2. Though Montefiore/Loewe suggest it 'may mean ... that he is too lazy to work, or too sensitive to accept gift' (MONTEFIORE & LOEWE, *op. cit.*, p.426).

In order to examine these texts more closely, they have been laid out in tabular form, broken into various sections that roughly correspond.

Each has been assigned a code for easier reference and the first of two versions from *K'tubot* 57b has been used as the base as it offers the most comprehensive treatment of the subject matter, This does not imply, however, that this was the source for all the others,[1] nor that this is the most reliable version from whichever initial source these ideas may have originated. The section of *Sifre* involving R. Y'hudah is repeated as it may relate to either of two traditions.

---

1. This version also contains Amoraic comments on the Tannaitic *baraitot* presented. These are also quoted as they shed some light on the texts we are comparing. These are shown in parenthesis { } to differentiate them from the Tannaitic material.

The illustration above is a of an antique *ts'dakah* (charity) box.

Sifre to D'varim 15:8	Tosefta Pe'ah 4:12-13 (TP)	Midrash Tannaim to D'varim 15:8 (MTD)
	האומר איני מתפרנס משל אחרים שוקדין עליו ומפרנסין אותו ונותנין לו לשום מלוה וחוזרין ונותנין לו לשום מתנה דר"מ (4:12)	והעבט תעביטנו אין לי אלא שאין לו ואינו רוצה להתפרנס
והעבט תעביטנו נותנים לו וחוזרים וממשכנים אותו דברי ר' יהודה	וחכמים או' נותנים לשום מלוה וחוזרין ונותנים לו לשום מתנה (4:12)	

OR

והעבט תעביטנו נותנים לו וחוזרים וממשכנים אותו	האומ' איני מתפרנס משל עצמי שוקדין עליו ומפרנסין אותו ונותנין לו לשם מתנה וחוזרין וגובין לו לשום מלוה (4:13)	יש לו ואין רוצה להתפרנס מנ'ין ת"ל תעביטנו מכל מקום
דברי ר' יהודה		אין לו ואינו רוצה להתפרנס אומרים לו הבא משכון וטול כדי שתזוח דעתו עליו
וחכמים אומ' אומרים לו הבא משכון כדי להגיס דעתו	ר' שמעון או' אומרין לו הבא משכון כדי לגוס את דעתו (4:12)	

60

K'tubot 57b (K1)	K'tubot 57b (K2)	Bava M'tsiah 31b (BM)
תנו רבנן אין לו ואינו רוצה להתפרנס נותנין לו לשום הלואה וחוזרין ונותנין לו לשום מתנה דברי ר' מאיר	ת"ר העבט זה שאין לו ואינו רוצה להתפרנס, שנותנים לו לשום הלואה וחוזרין ונותנין לו לשום מתנה	העבט תעביטנו אין לי אלא שאין לו ואינו רוצה להתפרנס אמר רחמנא תן לו דרך הלואה
וחכמים אומרים נותנין לו לשום מתנה וחוזרין ונותנין לו לשום הלואה		
{לשום מתנה הא לא שקיל אמר רבא לפתוח לו לשום מתנה}		
יש לו ואינו רוצה להתפרנס נותנין לו לשום מתנה וחוזרין ונפרעין ממנו	תעביטנו זה שיש לו ואינו רוצה להתפרנס שנותנין לו לשום מתנה וחוזרין ונפרעין הימנו	יש לו ואינו רוצה להתפרנס מנין תלמוד לומר תעביטנו מכל מקום
{חוזרין ונפרעין הימנו תו לא שקיל אמר רב פפא לאחר מיתה}	לאחר מיתה דברי ר' יהודה	
ר"ש אומר יש לו ואינו רוצה להתפרנס אין נזקקין לו	וחכ"א יש לו ואינו רוצה להתפרנס אין נזקקין לו ואלא מה אני מקיים תעביטנו דברה תורה כלשון בני אדם	ולר"ש דאמר יש לו ואינו רוצה להתפרנס אין נזקקין לו תעביטנו למה לי דברה תורה כלשון בני אדם
אין לו ואינו רוצה להתפרנס אומרים לו הבא משכון וטול כדי שתזוח דעתו עליו		

Sifre to *D'varim* 15:8	*Tosefta Pe'ah* 4:12-13 (TP)	*Midrash Tannaim* to *D'varim* 15:8 (MTD)
	One who says I do not want to support myself from that of others, we watch over him and support him, and we give to him as a loan and [then] return and give to him as a gift - the words of R. Meir.	'And you will surely lend him'. I know this only of one who does not have [adequate resources] but does not want to be supported [from gifts of *T'sdakah*] ...
'You will surely lend him', [implying] we give to him and [then] return and take a pledge from take a pledge from him - the words of R. Y'hudah.	But the Sages say we give to him as a gift and [then] return and give to as a loan.	

OR

| **'you will surely lend him', [implying] we give to him and [then] return and take a pledge from him ...** | One who says I do not want to support myself from my own [resources], we watch over him and support him and give to him as a gift and [then]return and give to him as a loan. | ... from where [do we learn this applies to] one who has [resources] and does not want to support himself [with them]. Scripture says 'you will surely lend him', in all cases. |
| **... the words of R. Y'hudah.** | | |

Bava M'tsiah 31b (BM)	*K'tubot* 67b (K2)	*K'tubot* 67b (K1)
'You will surely lend' I know this only of one who doesn't have [adequate resources] but does not want to be supported. The *Torah* [lit, the merciful] says "Give to him by way of loan ...	Our Rabbis taught 'lend' - this is one who doesn't have [adequate resources] but does not want to be supported, that we give to him as a loan and [then] return and give to him as a gift.	Our Rabbis taught 'lend' - this is one who doesn't have [adequate resources] but does not want to be supported, that we give to him as a loan and [then] return and give to him as a gift - the words of R. Meir.
		But the Sages say we give to him as a gift and [then] return and give to as a loan.
		{'As a gift'? But surely he would not take it. Rava said, [rather the Sages mean that they initially] open [the conversation] with him as [if it is] a gift.}
... from where [do we learn this applies to] one who has [resources] and does not want to support himself [from them receives *Ts'dakah*]. Scripture says 'you will surely lend him', in all cases.	'you will lend him' this is one who has [resources] but does not want to support himself [from them]. We give to him as a gift and [then] return and collect [payment] from him ...	He has [resources] but does not want to support himself [from them]. We give to him as a gift and [then] return and collect [payment] from him.
		{'Return and collect [payment] from him'? Surely he will not take again. Rav Pappa said, [rather they will collect] after his death.}
	... after his death - the words of R. Y'hudah.	

Sifre to *D'varim* 15:8 (SD)	Tosefta Pe'ah 4:12-13 (TP)	*Midrash Tannaim* to *D'varim* 15:8 (MTD)
And the Sages say, say to him, "Bring a pledge", in order to embolden his spirit.	R. Shim'on says, we say to him, "Bring a pledge", in order to embolden his spirit.	

Bava M'tsiah 31b (BM)	*K'tubot* 67b (K2)	*K'tubot* 67b (K1)
But R. Shim'on said, [if] he has [resources] but doesn't want to support himself, we are not obligated to [support] him.	But the Sages say, [if] he has [resources] but doesn't want to support himself, we are not obligated to [support] him.	R. Shim'on says, [if] he has [resources] but doesn't want to support himself, we are not obligated to [support] him.
Why then [does Scripture say] 'you will lend him'? The *Torah* speaks in the language of man.	If so, then how do I apply 'you will lend him'? The *Torah* speaks in the language of man.	
		And [for one who] does not want to be supported we say to him "Bring a pledge and take", in order to cheer his spirit.

All five parallel texts to our *Sifre* text commence with the case of the poor person with a valid claim on the community. All except MTD (which makes no comment on the order of presentation) suggest initially that this is presented as a loan and K1, K2 and TP inform us that the poor person is told subsequently that it is a gift. This would imply that there is no real intention to ever collect on the loan and so בדרך הלוה (by way of a loan) or לשום הלואה (in the name of a loan) is merely a mimicking of the normal procedure, reinforcing the view that when *Sifre* reports כמלוה (<u>as</u> a loan), it is only for the <u>sake of appearances</u>, In K1 and TP this view is attributed to the *Tanna*, R. Meir, and the term רחמנא (Merciful One) used in BM implies that the *Torah* itself takes the view that it should be presented as a loan. Clearly none of these sources initially lend support to R. Y'hudah's view, in *Sifre*, that it is first presented as a gift.

K1 and TP, however, do offer a dissenting view from that of R. Meir, both presented in the name of the Sages, but which agrees with the order that R. Y'hudah is suggesting. This may imply that their view originated from him. Normally the Sages view would indicate the majority opinion but here, one could argue that this does not seem to be the case. Indeed their opinion that one gives *ts'dakah* as a gift first seems odd given the general agreement to preserve the dignity of the poor. Moreover, if we were to accept the view of the Sages, then the case of the legitimate poor person would not differ from the case of the person who has resources as presented in K1, K2 and TP. In which case why would the distinction have been made in these texts?

Further, the Sages' view does not go unnoticed by the *Amora*, Rava who questions its validity. His attempt in K1 at reconciling the views is to suggest that the Sages mean לפתוח לו לשום מתנה (to open to him in the name of a gift) the emphasis being on '<u>to open</u>', in that this is a very initial approach where one does not yet know how the person will react.[1]

---

1. The Soncino translation of *K'tubot* 67b, suggests 'in the first instance as a gift'

Thus we can see that there is some considerable disagreement over how the approach is to be made to the deserving poor person.[1]

Before passing on to the other case, also worthy of comment are the variant readings concerning the pledge that is asked of the poor person. TP attributes this idea to R. Shim'on b. Yochai,[2] though in K1 and SD these are presented in the name of the Sages. K1 differs slightly in that it states that הבא משכון וטול (bring a pledge and [then] take), which might be taken to imply that the pledge was a real requirement and that the poor person is only allowed to take funds after doing so.[3] However this view is not supported by Rashi who states that, שיאמר אין לי משכון והם יאמרו טול בלא משכון ([if] he said, I do not have a pledge, they [nonetheless] say take, without a pledge).[4] It seems clear that even when presented as a loan, 'that they do not try to collect on it'[5] The pledge is not for the benefit of the lender. Rather it is all part of the pretence, להגיס את דעתו (to embolden his spirit).[6]

(Soncino Hebrew-English Ed.).
1. *Toldot Adam* also attempts to reconcile the view of the Sages by suggesting that,
   פתחו לו תחלה שיקבל לשום מתנה ולא רצה ובזה נתוודע שאינו רוצה להתפרנס ואז נותנים לו לשום הלואה
   (they opened to him in the beginning, that he would receive as a gift, [but if] he did not want [this], by this it would be known that he didn't want to be supported [this way], and then they gave him in the name of a loan). But,
   פשמעז נתוודע להגבאי שאינו רוצה להתפרנס ... נותנים לו לעולם לשום הלואה
   (from when it becomes known to the *gabbay* [charity distributor] that he does not want to be [thus] supported ... they always give him as a loan).
2. 3rd generation *Tanna*, see STRACK & STEMBERGER, *op. cit.*, p.84.
3. Finkelstein notes one reading of *Sifre* that gives וטול (and take(FINKELSTEIN, *op. cit.*, p.175)). Similarly Lieberman gives a variant reading for the *Tosefta* that also has the word.
4. Rashi s.v. שתזוח דעתו עליו (*K'tubot* 67b).
5. MOORE, *op. cit.*, p.167.
6. Montefiore & Loewe translates 'so as to quiet his mind' (MONTEFIORE & LOEWE, *op. cit.*, p.422).

More importantly the statement in K1, הבא משכון וטול (Bring a pledge and [then] take), suggests that the funds were not given until after the pretence of the loan was over and thus it was not presented as a gift first. This would support the contention that, והחכמים אומרים לו הבא משכון in *Sifre* implies 'but the Sages say, we [present as a loan initially and] say to him, "Bring a pledge!"', and that they are disagreeing with R. Y'hudah's order of presentation.

דעת can be variously translated as knowledge, mind, temperament, physical disposition, constitution, opinion or even intention[1] but given the context a mental attitude seems implied. להגיס is from the root גוס (to swell, embolden),[2] though in variant *Sifre* texts we find להפיס (to break a persons anger, to pacify or to comfort),[3] and in K1 it suggests כדי שתזוח דעתו עליו (in order that his spirits be cheered within [lit. upon] him).[4] Attention to the mental well-being of the poor person was as important to the *Tannaim* as much as attention to his physical needs; such a high priority was the avoidance of shame in their dealings.

Thus far we have looked solely at the case of the person who, in the eyes of the Rabbis, was considered to have a legitimate claim on charitable funds, since it is this case only that appears to be present in the *Sifre* text. The other texts presented, however, also look at the case of one who has resources to maintain himself but does not wish to do so.

---

1. JASTROW, *op. cit.*, p.316.
2. *Ibid.*, p.225.
3. *Ibid.*, p.1166.
4. *Ibid.*, p.385. Rashi explains here that,

יגבה לבו לומר דעתם לחזור ולגבות הימני הואיל ותבעוני משכון אין זו
הלואה ויטול בלא בושה

(he will strengthen his heart by saying [to himself] it is their intention to return and collect from me [for] since they demanded a pledge, this is only a loan, and he [therefore] will take without shame).

The concern of these texts appears to be to demonstrate a reason for the apparently superfluous repetition of the verb עבט seen in the infinite absolute of the *hiphil* form[1] העבט תעביטנו (you will surely lend him). The repetition is used to suggest that the 'undeserving' applicant is also supported, even though one might think otherwise. TP even goes as far as saying that we should be so concerned that שוקדין עליו (we watch over him carefully), as would be the case of the 'deserving' poor.

All the other texts (again excluding MTD) appear to agree that they give to the 'undeserving' applicant first as a gift and then convert it into a loan, which <u>will be collected</u> later on, whereas payment would not have been exacted from a genuine poor person.

Of particular interest here, is that this view is presented in the name of R. Y'hudah in K2 and this is also the order that he prescribes for the giving of *ts'dakah* in our *Sifre* text, which had appeared to contradict the *Baraita* that had preceded it in *Sifre*, This has led *Toldot Adam*, *Emek Han'tsiv*, Rabbeynu Hillel and the GR"A to all suggest that the *Sifre* text is <u>incomplete</u> and that it should read, נותנים לו וחוזרים וממשכנים אותו לאחר מיתה דברי ר' יהודה (we give to him and return and take a pledge from him for [collection] after his death - the words of R. Y'hudah) and therefore that this view only applies in the case of one who has resources. This attempt at harmonisation implies that the *Sifre* text is somehow defective and is a vestige of a fuller form, perhaps seen in K2. However, in *Sifre* we read וממשכנים (and we take a pledge) whereas in K1 and K2 it gives ונפרעין (and we collect it) which might support our initial contention that R. Y'hudah's view refers to the deserving applicant. Alternatively

---

1. Indeed the reason for the apparent repetition of the section within *K'tubot* 67b is that K1 (like TP) is an apodictic halachic passage, stating the law without Scriptural support whereas K2 (like BM, *Sifre* and MTD) are midrashically derived from the verse. In the final redaction both traditions have been included side by side.

Sifre may have been changed by the redactor, who faced with an incomplete tradition made it reflect the discussion on the משכון (pledge) that followed.[1]

It does not end there, for as with the case of the 'deserving' poor there is also dissent. Here, though, it is not concerning the order of presentation, rather as to whether one should give at all.

In K1 and BM, R. Shim'on, and in K2, the Sages[2] quote a dictum much favoured by the school of R. Yishma'el that,

דברי תורה כלשון בני אדם (the Torah speaks in the language of man) 'who [is] in the habit of repeating [his] words [and] hence no inference can be drawn from the repetition in the text cited'.[3] Therefore they conclude that, יש לו ואינו רוצה להתפרנס אין נזקקין לו ([if] he has [resources] but does not wish to support himself, one is not obligated towards him).

In summary, though there is a level of disagreement amongst the texts, from a detailed examination of the cases outlined, one could conclude the following. Generally the *Tannaim* appear to suggest that if one knows the person to be of good family or if one has had previous dealings, one opens the conversation as if you are giving a loan, requesting a pledge to preserve the dignity of the recipient. There seems to be no intention that the loan be paid back, since one then quickly returns to state that it is, in fact, a gift.

If, however, one comes across a new person, one suggests a gift in initial conversation but if rebuffed, one immediately responds by

---

1. Given the discussion in K1 does not appear to have been aware of the tradition in K2, it may be that Rav Pappa's explanation that they collect only after death in K1 has been projected back on to the *Tanna*, R. Y'hudah at a later stage in K2, in order to give Pappa's view some support.
2. Which suggests that R. Shim'on's view became the majority opinion.
3. *K'tubot* 67b, Soncino Hebrew-English Ed., note c (5).

suggesting a loan as more appropriate, and the same procedure then applies.

If the person was considered undeserving, having resources, opinion seems to be split between giving the person a gift and then collecting after death from the estate, or not giving at all.

Our *Sifre* text does not make the distinction between the two cases and is generally simpler.[1] It does show the need to open with words to either determine what the approach should be or to ask the person whether they need a loan. It also explains the reason for the pledge. The main area of difficulty with the text is the view of R. Y'hudah as it may represent a disagreement with R. Meir as to the order one presents *ts'dakah* to the deserving poor person, or, as seems more likely is a statement of how one should deal with an undeserving applicant, which is perhaps incomplete and taken out of its original context.

---

1. The GR"A amends this section of text quite considerably, adding in much of the material from the parallel texts regarding the deserving and undeserving poor. By this he perhaps suggests that the *Sifre* text is deficient, though this is not necessarily the case.

Section 6 - 'which is lacking for him'

די מחסורו אי אתה מצווה להעשירו אשר יחסר לו אפי׳ סוס ואפי׳ עבד ומעשה בהלל הזקן שנתן לעני בן טובים סוס אחד שהיה מתעמל בו ועבד אחד שהוא משמשו שוב מעשה בגליל העליון שהיו מעלים לאדם ליטרא בשר של צפור בכל יום לו זו אשה כענין שנ׳ אעשה לו עזר כנגדו

('Sufficient for his lack' - you are not commanded to make him rich. 'Which is lacking for him'; even a horse and even a slave. [There was] a case of Hillel the Elder[1] that he gave to a certain poor person, [who was] of good family, a horse that he [the poor person, previously] was wont to exercise with[2] and a slave that [previously] he was wont to have serve him.[3] Furthermore, [there was] a case in Upper Galilee that they used to bring to a guest a *litra* of meat each day. 'For him' this is a wife, in accordance with the idea, as it is said 'I will make for him a helpmate').

The initial concern here for the *Tannaim* is how they might understand די (enough, sufficient) in order that they be able to determine how much and what to give.[4]

---

1. See STRACK & STEMBERGER, *op. cit.*, p.71 for details about this important Pharisaic teacher.
2. *Hitpa'el form*, see JASTROW, *op. cit.*, p.1089. Hammer renders 'a horse to exercise upon' (HAMMER, *op. cit.*, p. 162). Or possibly 'to work upon' from עמל (to labour, take pains (JASTROW, *op. cit.*, p.1088)). Neusner translates as 'a horse with which to work' (NEUSNER, *op. cit.*, p.290).
3. The translation supplied here reflects later discussion in this section.
4. Posner suggests, however, that the advice '"you are required to maintain him but not to enrich him" [is based on the sages] stressing the word "need"' (POSNER, *op.*

As is apparent from their detailed discussions, the *Tannaim* preferred a systematic approach to the giving of *ts'dakah* so that, as Hartman and Marx point out, 'the scriptural "mighty stream of righteousness" [*Amos* 5:24 was converted into the talmudic "half a *kab* or 12 eggs volume of bread".[1] די in the eyes of the Sages, would seem to be imprecise terminology and therefore raises the question, <u>'what is enough'</u>?

Their first reaction is to interpret the word from the point of view of the giver, in that אין אתה מצוה להעשרו (you are not commanded to make him rich).

This implies that one is only commanded to give him 'enough' to maintain him, a sentiment that emerges more clearly in the Talmudic statement, that,

תנו רבנן די מחסרו אתה מצווה עליו לפרנסו ואי אתה מצווה עליו לעשרו

(our Rabbis taught 'sufficient from his lack' [implies that] you are commanded concerning him <u>to support him</u>, but you are not commanded concerning him to make him rich).[2] *Midrash Tannaim* explains that,

אתה מצווה עליו להחיותו ואין אתה מצווה עליו לעשרו (you are commanded concerning him to <u>keep him alive</u> [i.e. to provide enough to sustain him) but you are not commanded to make him rich).[3]

The minimum requirement is thus made quite plain by the *Tannaim*.[4]

---

cit., p.171), rather than די (sufficient/enough). It is more likely that the Sages are looking at the words in combination rather than in isolation.
1. HARTMAN, D & MARX, T, *Charity*, from *Contemporary Jewish Religious Thought*, Ed. COHEN, A & MENDES-FLOHR, P, Free Press, New York, 1988, p.49.
2. *K'tubot* 67a.
3. *Midrash Tannaim* to *D'varim* 15:8.
4. Moore understands this as meaning that you do not have 'to make him better off than he was before' (MOORE, *op. cit.*, p.116), whilst Rambam understands it, in light of what follows in the Scriptural verse as,

The emphasis in the *Sifre* text, however, quickly turns from the giver to the needy person themselves and the word די takes on new meaning which, as we will see by reference to the case examples provided, will lead us to read it instead as 'matched to' or 'appropriate to circumstances', This is brought about through their interpretation of the verb חסר (missing/lacking) linked with the key word לו (to him).

חסר implies a lessening, a diminishing of some kind, from a previous state.[1] Its use also conveys that the material things that are needed by the poor are by rights already their possessions, but are merely 'temporarily' missing from them. Since 'the poor man's right to food, clothing and shelter is considered by Judaism as a legal claim',[2] the giving of *ts'dakah* is perceived as the restoration of the true balance and as such is an act of social justice rather than mere philanthropic sentiment. This is very much in accordance with both the Scriptural and Rabbinic interpretation of the 'gifts' to the poor.

Referring to לו, Posner explains "... for his need which he wanteth", the accent being on "his" and "he"',[3] and for this reason the *Tannaim* argue that *ts'dakah* has to be given with the individual circumstances of the poor person in mind.[4] This focus on לו is important as without it we would face the same apparent confusion as Neusner. His translation of אשר יחסר לו as 'whatever he needs'[5] prompts him to suggest that the

---

ומצוה אתה להשלים חסרנו ואין אתה מצוה לערו (and you are commanded to <u>restore [make complete] his lack</u> and you are not [commanded] to make him rich (*Mishneh Torah, Hilchot Mat'not Aniyim* 7:3)).
1. JASTROW, *op. cit.*, p.489.
2. Ed. BIRNBAUM, P, *Mishneh Torah*, Hebrew Publishing Co., New York, 1989, p.157.
3. POSNER, *op. cit.*, p.171.
4. Hirsch, however, argues that 'according to the *Sifri*, lit is] the רבוי [i.e. פתח תפתח נתן תתן [that] ... extends the manner in which the duty has to be performed, making it necessary to adjust one's assistance in accordance with the requirements of each particular case'. (HIRSCH *op. cit.*, p.271).
5. NEUSNER, *op. cit.*, p. 290.

Sifre statement that 'you are not commanded to make him rich' is then supposedly 'contradicted' by the cases that follow, since they appear to be suggesting that you give the needy person such apparent symbols of wealth as a horse, a slave and a pound of meat each day.[1]

Though there may be some tension between the statements, it is arguable that the two cases are not the extreme or contradictory examples that Neusner posits, and that in neither case do they make the recipient rich. An examination of the parallel text in *Tosefta Pe'ah*, shows that the two cases involving Hillel and the men of Upper Galillee follow a section[2] that is quite clearly concerned with demonstrating that appropriate *ts'dakah* is given, based on what is lacking to a particular individual,

היה משתמש בכלי מילת נתנין לו כלי מילת מעה נתנין לו מעה עיסה נתנין לו עיסה פת נתנין לו פת להאכילו בתוך פיו מאכילין בתוך פיו שנאמר די מחסרו אשר יחסר לו אפי׳ עבד סוס ...

([if] he was wont to use woollen apparel, we give him woollen apparel, a *m'ah*[3] (coin), we give him a *m'ah* (coin), a measure of flour,[4] we give

---

1. Hartman and Marx consider this to be 'radical' and that it is an 'indulgence of the pauper in some degree of conspicuous consumption to help maintain his facade of self sufficiency' (HARTMAN & MARX, *op. cit.*, p. 53), though the key here is still the avoidance of shame and not mere pampering of the poor person.
2. This section appears later in our *Sifre* text, though slightly shorter and in a different order, and more importantly appended to a different verse (*D'varim* 15:11), where the *Tannaim* felt there was a need to explain why different terms for poor were used. The *Sifre* text reads,

   פתך תפתח את ידך לאחיך לאביונך למה נאמרו כולם הרואי ליתן לו פת נותנים לו פת עיסה נתנים לו עיסה מעה נתנים לו מעה להאכילו בתוך פיו מאכילים בתוך פיו

   ('you will surely open your hand to your brother, to your poor [and] to your needy'. Why does it say all of these [categories]? [It teaches that if] it is fitting to give him a piece of bread we give him a piece of bread, a measure of flour, we give him a measure of flour, a *m'ah* [coin] we give him a *m'ah*, [or if the need is] to place food in his mouth, we place food in his mouth). See section 15.
3. The lowest denomination silver coin, one sixth of a dinar. See CARMELL, A, *Aiding Talmud Study*, Feldheim 1991, p.82.
4. 'A quantity of flour used for one person's meal', JASTROW, *op. cit.*, p.1072.

him a measure of flour, a piece of bread, we give him a piece of bread, [if the need is] to place food in his mouth, we place food into his mouth, as it says 'appropriate to his lack which is lacking to him', even a horse, even a slave ...).[1] This then leads into the two cases cited. There is clearly no hint of the provision of excessive wealth here, only the balancing of lack with appropriate action.

Aside from its appending to a different verse, and the mention of clothing provision for the poor, the main difference between the *Tosefta* passage and that quoted in *Sifre* is the use of היה משתמש (he was wont to use) as opposed to הראוי ליתן (if it is fitting to give).[2] Arguably the former centres firmly on the requirements of the needy person, whilst the latter is allowing the giver to make some judgement as to interpreting those requirements. Nonetheless, how would a person know what is fitting? Only by reference to the needy person. Thus in both instances the overwhelming theme of the passage is to demonstrate that one should consider the individual circumstances of the needy person. For one who was previously well off what he lacks when poor will be considerably different from someone who has always known hardship. Therefore 'you should consider his social status and if it demands, give him a horse for riding and a slave to run before him'.[3]

With this in mind, the episodes with Hillel and the men of Upper Galilee, do not appear as extreme as Neusner suggests. Indeed, as we shall see, they are wholly appropriate to the circumstances.

Taking the Hillel case initially, (though many of the lessons learnt apply equally to the other), the key to understanding the intention of the *Tannaim* in bringing the מעשה (lit. deed, but implying a case precedent),[4] is that the *ts'dakah* being given in this instance is being

---

1. *Tosefta Pe'ah* 4: 10.
2. *Sifre* to *D'varim* 15:11.
3. MONTEFIORE & LOEWE, *op, cit.*, p.425.
4. 'The citation of an actual happening on which a decision is reported' (CARMELL,

directed towards an עני בן טובים (poor person of good family).

We have already noted this term in our study, but without explanation. Montefiore and Loewe suggest that this term refers to 'a son of goodly folk, gentry, born of noble descent'[1] and thus is someone who was used to better circumstances and has fallen on hard times. Similarly Moore speaks of one 'who in his better days was accustomed to luxury'.[2] Maccoby, however, sees this as implying only to 'public respectability and honour' and possibly not to previous wealth.[3]

That this phrase is employed rather than אביון (the subject of the Biblical text), or even just עני (poor [person]), without any further clarification, points to the Rabbis' concern to ensure that this מעשה still reflected the ideal of suitable or appropriate giving rather than any overly extreme case.

As well as its appearance in *Tosefta Pe'ah* 4:10 the tale also appears in *Y'rushalmi Pe'ah* 8:7 both with very little variant from the *Sifre* text. The most significant is the use of נתן (gave) in the *Sifre* text as opposed to לקח (took [for]) in the *Tosefta* and the *Y'rushalmi*, which perhaps implies that in the former it was an outright gift, whilst in the latter two texts it may have only been a temporary transaction.[4]

---

op. cit., p.72). Also see STRACK AND STEMBERGER, *op. cit.*, p.52 for discussion of the terminology.
1. MONTEFIORE & LOEWE, *op. cit.*, p.425.
2. MOORE, *op. cit.*, p.166.
3. MACCOBY, *op. cit.*, p.86.
4. The Soncino English-Hebrew Ed. translates לקח as 'bought' in the version to be found in *K'tubot* 67a, whilst noting that Alfasi renders 'he hired', which would accord with the idea of a temporary transaction. See section 5 for discussion on gifts and loans. The other variation between the texts centres around the placing of the word אחד (one), i.e. whether this refers to the עני בן טובים (poor person of good family) or the סוס (horse).

The case as reported in *Midrash Tannaim* adds further clarification, stating that, הכל לפי כבודו אפילו סוס לרכוב עליו ועבד לרוץ לפניו ([it is] all according to his honour, even a horse to ride upon and a slave to run before him).[1] The avoidance of shame is brought forward again as an important factor in the giving of *ts'dakah* and according to this version, at least, the reason for treating the עני בן טובים with such care and consideration.

That this reason is given in *Midrash Tannaim* may support Maccoby's contention that עני בן טובים was a phrase denoting previous status regarding a person's honour and position within the community rather than it being solely determined by that person's previous level of wealth.

It is, perhaps by comparison of our text with the variant found in *K'tubot* 67b which best demonstrates the original intention of the *Sifre* text, and indicates how this intention may have been 'corrupted' by later amplification.[2] It reads,
אמרו אליו על הלל הזקן שלקח לעני בן טובים אחד סוס לרכוב עליו ועבד לרוץ לפניו פעם אחד לא מצא עבד לרוץ לפניו ורץ לפניו שלשה מילין
(they [the Sages] said of Hillel the elder, that he bought for a poor

---

1. *Midrash Tannaim* to *D'varim* 15:8.
2. Because of the difficulty of dating individual traditions within the context of their larger works, it is possible that what is seen as amplification in *K'tubot* 67b is actually an earlier and fuller version of the tale from which the others have drawn, but given its later general date and the treatment given to the other מעשה concerning the people of Upper Galilee in the same section, it is more likely that this is an enhancement of the *Sifre/Tosefta/Y'rushalmi* version. 'Because the frequency of narrative material increases with the temporal distance from a particular Rabbi one must expect later inventions and embellishments' (STRACK AND STEMBERGER, *op. cit.*, p.67) but 'it depends on the text's individual genre and its functions ... whether the development leads to a constant embellishment ... or rather to a polishing and shortening ... it is impossible to generalise about whether a short form is earlier or later' (*ibid.*, p44).

person, son of good [family], a horse, to ride upon and a slave to run before him. On one occasion he [Hillel] did not find a slave to run before him and [so] he ran before him [for] three *milin*).[1]

The tale appears to have been extended and there are a couple of particularly striking changes from the *Sifre* text. These seem to indicate a movement away from presenting this case purely as an example of matching *ts'dakah* to the poor person's circumstance, towards using it to show the lengths to which the great Hillel would go.

In the *K'tubot* variant, the horse is provided so that the poor person is able לרכוב עליו (to ride upon it) in the earlier texts, *Sifre* included, the horse is provided so שהיה מתעמל בו, which may mean 'that he exercised upon' or perhaps, 'that he would work upon'. Whilst supplying a horse merely for riding could be viewed as an ostentatious luxury, without which the poor person would not suffer much hardship, the *Sifre* text at least suggests that the horse, was actually <u>provided for a purpose</u>; to meet a genuine need.

Further, whereas in *Sifre* it says of the slave שהיה משמשו (that he served him), the apparent embellishment of *K'tubot* links the slave to the provision of the horse, in that his sole reported purpose becomes לרוץ לפניו (to run before him [the poor person]). Providing a slave to serve someone of good family, who has fallen on hard times, would seem reasonable and 'appropriate', doing so merely to provide a runner again does seem a little more extravagant (even though he may have been used to this previously).

It is, however, the main addition to the tale, that of Hillel running before the poor person, that has perhaps prompted Neusner to feel that this case is a very extreme example. There is perhaps an indication that the Sages at work in *K'tubot*, did not feel that the tale as it appears in

---

1. One *mil* = 2,000 cubits, approximately one kilometre (CARMELL, *op.cit.*, p.77).

Sifre was strong enough to convey the lengths one should go to.[1]

Hartman and Marx suggest that 'Hillel fulfilled the norm of zedakah by acting as a chauffeur for a poor person who had previously been wealthy',[2] but arguably what we have in the *Sifre* text represents the 'norm', and what we have in *K'tubot* is an elaboration not necessarily designed to promote the idea of meeting the needs of each pauper defined by his own history, temperament or habits,[3] but rather, it seems, to increase the glory of Hillel's deed.

It is also worth noting that a tradition quoted in the New Testament also links the idea of giving charity to the poor with that of travelling with someone for a distance. Matthew 5:41 states, 'and whoever shall compel thee to go a mile, go with him twain' immediately in conjunction with verse 42 which states, 'give to him that asketh thee, and from him that would borrow of thee turn thou not away'. Perhaps the Sages recounting the tale in *K'tubot* wished to see Hillel go one better![4]

Certainly, 'the 'biographical' narratives about the Rabbis are ... mostly ... relatively late texts intended for edification, exhortation and political ends'[5] rather than true reports of that Sage's life. This, is 'especially true of Hillel whose accounts are very strongly reminiscent of Hellenistic cliches (*chria*)'.[6]

---

1. Something that the Sages developed even further with the example concerning Upper Galillee. It is also possible that the *Bavli* version is focusing mainly on the idea of the honour due to such a poor person, whilst the *Sifre* version is concerned more with fulfilling their practical needs.
2. HARTMAN & MARX, *op. cit.*, p.51.
3. *Ibid.*, p.52.
4. As Urbach notes, 'the charitable deeds of the Christian communities influenced ... the [Jewish] dicta evaluating charity and the practice of lovingkindness' (URBACH, *op. cit.*, p.439). Montefiore and Loewe also raise this possible link between Hillel's deed and Matthew 5:41-42 (MONTEFIORE & LOEWE, *op. cit.*, p.425).
5. STRACK & STEMBERGER, *op. cit.*, p.67.
6. *Ibid.*, p.68.

Finally, on the subject of סוס שהיה מתעמל בו, and ועבד היה משמשו, it can be argued that an alternative translation to 'a horse with which he exercised/worked' or 'a slave that was to serve him' may be more appropriate. Since היה with a participle 'is often used to express continuous action in the past',[1] the use of היה in *Sifre* could imply that he was <u>wont to do this previously</u>.[2] This would sit very well with our understanding of the עני בן טובים, who may indeed have been used to such luxuries before he fell into poverty, and hence a translation reflecting this has been adopted at the start of this section.

The second case, likewise reported in *Sifre*, *Tosefta* and the *Y'rushalmi* concentrates on one of the main 'gifts to the poor', that of food. The example is made 'special' in all instances by stressing that it was ליטרא בשר (a *litra*[3] of meat), and according to one *Sifre* variant[4]

---

1. CARMELL, *op. cit.*, p.60.
2. The commentary *Toldot Yitschak* to the *Y'rushalmi*, whilst viewing להתעמל as work rather than exercise, nonetheless suggests that this was a regular way of behaving, that, היינו לרכוב עליו ולעשות מלאכה בו וכו' שהיה רגיל כך (it was to ride upon and to do work with it etc. which he was used to [do]). Hirsch notes that such behaviour may 'be indispensible to him on account of habits formed in previous circumstances' (HIRSCH, *op. cit.*, p.271), Similar usage has already been seen in *Tosefta Pe'ah* 4: 10 with היה משתמש (he was wont to use/he was used to), and the Rambam in relating the case, similarly understands that,

   אפילו היה דרכו של זה העני לרכוב על הסוס ועבד רץ לפניו והעני ירד מנכסיו קונין לו סוס לרכוב עליו ועבד לרוץ לפניו

   (even if it was the way of this poor person to ride upon a horse whilst a slave ran before him - and the poor person lost his possessions, we acquire for him a horse to ride upon and a slave to run before him (*Mishneh Torah, Hilchot Mat'not Aniyim* 7:3)).
3. 'Both a weight, the Roman *libra*, and a measure of capacity' (*K'tubot* 67b, Soncino Hebrew-English Ed., note a(9)). Also referred to as a *maneh*, roughly the equivalent of one pound, CARMELL, *op. cit.*, p.81.
4. דפוס ויניציה ש״ה - the Venice manuscript, FINKELSTEIN, *op. cit.*, p.175.

בשר של צפור, (fowl, probably chicken)[1] provided בכל יום (every day).

Given the prevailing economic circumstances, this would have placed a not inconsiderable burden on the community, However, this still may have been 'appropriate' depending on the nature of the recipient, and it is on this subject that the main variation in the texts occurs. Different manuscripts of *Sifre* variously report that the meat was given לאורח (to a guest), לעני בן טובים or merely לאדם (to a man).[2] Both the *Tosefta* and *Y'rushalmi* versions give לזקן אחד (to an old person).

The general description therefore (with the exception of לאדם) is that of someone who would necessarily command a greater deal of respect than normal; the guest, because of the emphasis the Jews place on hospitality, the old man because of the respect due to one's elders and the עני בן טובים because this is what he would have been used to in the past. Perhaps this idea of respect is also conveyed by the use of the *hiphil* form מעלים (lit. brought up) to him, rather than simply נתן (gave).[3]

Unlike the Hillel case, where it is not altogether certain, the amplification of the Upper Galillee example in *K'tubot* 67b, is without doubt an embellishment by later Sages who are discussing the merits of the deed. The premise is similar, with the poor man identified specifically as an עני בן טובים to match the Hillel example, but

---

1. *Tosefta Pe'ah* 4:10 gives בשר בצפורי which Lieberman explains as meaning 'a [*litra*] of flesh [according] to the measure used in Sepphoris' and *Y'rushalmi Pe'ah* 8:7 בשר צפורים (flesh of birds). *Toldot Yitschak* explains this as בשר עוף (chicken meat) in line with how it is interpreted by the Sages in *K'tubot* 67b.
2. The full listing of variant readings given in *Sifre* is shown in Finkelstein's critical apparatus, see FINKELSTEIN, *op, cit.*, p175.
3. Though this verb may also have been used because the guest may have been served in an upper room.

through faulty transmission the reference to the meat being from a צפור (bird) or בצפורי (according to the Sepphoris measure) has been transformed into an identification of the poor person himself as being from צפורי (Sepphoris), a town on one of the Upper Galilean mountains.

However what follows in *K'tubot* 67b is quite revealing,

ליטרא בשר מאי רבותא אמר רב הונא ליטרא בשר משל עוף ואיבעית אימא בליטרא בשר ממש רב אשי אמר התם כפר קטן היה בכל יומא הוא מפסדי חיותא אמטולתיה

(A *litra* of meat? What is the greatness [in this]?[1] R. Chuna[2] said [it was] a *litra* of meat from a fowl. And if you like, I can say, they purchased ordinary meat for a *litra* [of money]. R. Ashi[3] said in the case [just cited] it was a small village [and] every day a beast was spoilt for his sake).

From the very framing of the question מאי רבותא (lit. what is the greatness, i.e. what is so special about this teaching?) we might infer that the concern of the two Babylonian *Amoraim* is less to demonstrate that this was a suitable act of *ts'dakah*, and more to show that this was a great deed carried out by an earlier generation.

The meat is identified by R. Huna as chicken meat which as Rashi explains[4] was יקרים (expensive). Rashi explains of R. Ashi's view that it was a burden on the community since,

---

1. Though in Palestine after the Bar Kochba revolt, a *litra* of meat would have been a substantial quantity, in Babylonia the *Amoraim* would not necessarily have considered this to be the case. Thus they provide alternative explanations based on the quality (i.e. type) of the meat, the cost or the amount of wastage, rather than the quantity.
2. R. Huna, a 2nd generation Babylonian *Amora*, see STRACK & STEMBERGER, *op. cit.*, p.96.
3. A 6th generation Babylonian *Amora*, *ibid.*, p.107.
4. Rashi s.v. משל עופות (*K'tubot* 67b).

כפר קטן היה ואין המותר נמכר (it was a small village and [thus] there was no way to sell the remainder).[1] It is quite clear that through these Amoraic discussions there is a shift of emphasis, that focuses not on the person's requirements but on the glory of the giver and the act itself.

Though the original purpose of our particular case seems to have been 'subverted' a little by the *Amoraim, K'tubot* 67b does preserve another tradition about a *Tanna* which firmly emphasises the giving of suitable *ts'dakah* by showing the result of an occasion where appropriate charity was not given.

ההוא דאתא לקמיה דרבי נחמיה אמר ליה במה אתה סועד א"ל בבשר שמן ויין ישן רצונך שתגלגל עמי בעדשים גלגל עמו בעדשים ומת

([A certain man] came before R. Nechemyah[2] [to apply for *ts'dakah*]. [The Rabbi] said to him, what do you [normally] eat? [The man] said to him, fat meat and old wine. [R. Nechemyah said, do] you wish to put up with [subsisting] on lentils with me? He put up with lentils with him and died!)[3]

In contrast when the *Amora* Rava is approached under similar circumstances and questions another man that his demands of fat chicken and old wine might be a burden on the community the man explains that, שכל אחד ואחד נותן הקב"ה פרנסתו בעתו (that [for] everyone, the Holy One Blessed be He gives his support in [accordance with] his habits [lit. his time]).[4] Once again, the emphasis is on his individual needs, and miraculously Rava's sister arrives bearing fat chicken and old wine as if to confirm the statement.

---

1. *Ibid.*
2. A 3rd generation *Tanna*, see STRACK & STEMBERGER, *op. cit.*, p.85.
3. The text later apportions blame to the man whose lifestyle was too luxurious rather than any fault of R. Nechemyah.
4. *K'tubot* 67b.

Notwithstanding this 'miraculous confirmation', through all the examples above, there does seem to be a tension between giving luxurious items which match that individual's lack, and yet appear to make a person rich.

The final part of this section of *Sifre* also concentrates on the recipient, though, on this occasion, brings a new dimension to the word לו (to him).

Elsewhere this word will be interpreted very differently (see section 11), but here it is still very much part of the concept that *ts'dakah* should be appropriate. In a way, the exegesis provided is even more of an extreme case than the previous two in the lengths to which it suggests one should have to go to meet this objective, but is not queried by Neusner as it does not appear to contradict the idea of not making a person rich.

The prompt here for the Rabbis is an attempt to counter the seeming redundancy of לו, given that the Biblical text has already identified the subject of the verse by stating די מחסרו (appropriate to <u>his</u> lack).

By means of a *g'zerah shava*[1] the Rabbis link the לו of *D'varim* 15:8 to a its occurence in *B'reshit* 2:18. This hermeneutical technique in Midrashic exegesis is held to be very characteristic of the school of R. Akiva who would try to find meaning in every single word,[2] though it

---

1. 'Lit. 'equal ordinance' or 'statute' ... an argument made from analogy. Strictly speaking this is only to be used [as is the case here] if two given Torah statements make use of identical experessions.' (STRACK & STEMBERGER, *op. cit.*, p.21). Though the term is not specifically used, this is clearly an example.
2. 'R. Akiva used methods which included interpretation of every word ... and 'in general this is part of the tendency of the Tannaitic Midrashim to demonstrate the depedendence of the halakah on the written word ... every phrase of a verse, sometimes every word, is useful in teaching what has to be done' (HAMMER, *op. cit.*, p.8 and p.12). Modern scholarship however would suggest that the school of R. Yishma'el was no less prone to such exegesis.

does raise the question of, why out of all the many occurrences of the word לו in Scripture, why should the authors of *Sifre* centre on this particular one.[1]

Whilst it clearly does provide an example of matching what is lacking, even to the extent of finding a wife, it does seem a little out of place, After all, our text says prior to the detailed cases, אפילו סוס ואפילו עבד (even a horse and even a slave) it does not add 'and even a wife'. Moreover, in the *Y'rushalmi* version of the Hillel and Upper Galilee tales, it does not appear and in Tosefta *Pe'ah* 4:10 it appears 'sandwiched' uncomfortably between the statement אפילו סוס ואפילו עבד and the two tales.

It is almost as if the section has been appropriated from a separate tradition and added in alongside. This separate tradition is perhaps witnessed in *Tosefta K'tubot* 6:8 where it is part of an anonymous teaching which provides yet another explanation to the meaning behind די מחסרו אשר יחסר לו (appropriate to his lack which is lacking to him), an interpretation that shows the verse as it applies specifically to the case of the orphan.[2]

יתום שמבקש לישא שוכרין לו בית ומציעין מטה ואחר כך משיאין לו אשה שנ' די מחסרו אשר יחסר לו אפ' עבד אפ' סוס לו זו אשה שנ' להלן אעשה לו עזר כנגדו מה לו אמור להלן זו אשה אף לו אמור כאן אשה

(An orphan that seeks to marry, we rent for him a house, and we prepare for him a bed and after that we cause him to marry a wife, as it says 'appropriate from his lack which is lacking for him' even a horse

---

1. Maccoby, commenting on its occurrence in *Tosefta Pe'ah* 4:10, suggests that 'in this instance both passages ... contain the word *lo* which is a common enough word, but in these two cases the word seems to have a similar redundancy, so the verse in Deuteronomy is regarded as deliberately recalling the verse in Genesis' (MACCOBY, op. *cit.*, p. 136).
2. The orphan (along with the widow and the stranger) were specific recipients singled out by Scripture and by the Rabbis.

and even a slave. 'For him' this is a wife, as it says elsewhere [*B'reshit* 2:18] will make for him a helper corresponding to him'. What is 'for him'? Just as 'for him' [which is] said there [means] a wife, so 'for him' said here [means] a wife).

Even here, in the midst of dealing with the orphan, the horse and slave interpretation is not absent, which perhaps indicates a certain relationship between the two traditions.

Though the *g'zerah shavah* is explained carefully, the derivation from the phrase די מחסרו וכו (appropriate to his lack ...) to imply specifically a house and a table does seem a little tenuous,[1] and it may be this tradition is better preserved in *K'tubot* 67b which strengthens the link by stating,

ת"ר יתום שבא לישא שוכרין לו בית ומציעין מטה וכל כלי תשמישו ואחר כך משיאין לו אשה שנ' די מחסרו אשר יחסר לו די מחסרו זה הבית אשר יחסר זה מטה ושלחן לו זו אשה וכן הוא אומר אעשה לו עזר כנגדו

(our Rabbis taught, an orphan that comes [for assistance] to marry, we rent for him a house and prepare for him a bed and all the utensils for him to use and after that we cause him to marry a wife, as it says 'appropriate from his lack which lacking for him'. 'Appropriate from his lack' this [implies] the house, 'which is lacking', this [implies] the bed and table 'for him' this is a wife, and so it says 'I will make for him a helper corresponding to him').

The Sages have taken the tri-partite form of the verse and presented it in such a way to allow them to assign each section of the phrase to each

---

1. Silbermann notes that 'the derivation of the "wife" from the word לו in Gen. 11.18 is a mere אסמכתא [Scriptural text used retrospectively in support of a rabbinical enactment (see JASTROW, *op. cit.*, p.94)] [as is] the duty of providing the poor with a house [which] is deduced from די מחסרו and with furniture from אשר יחסר' (SILBERMANN, *op. cit.*, p.207).

individual act of *ts'dakah*, though one is left wondering why one section implies one act rather than another, as no further explanation is given.

It may be, therefore, that the redactor of *Sifre* when faced with this tradition specific to the orphan against the cases of giving to the עני בן טובים outlined in the Hillel and Upper Galilee examples rejected the house and bed in favour of the horse and slave, but retained the element containing the reference to *B'reshit* 2:18, as a means of dealing with the potential redundancy.

It is clear then that the general principle amongst the *Tannaim* is to ensure that *ts'dakah* should be <u>appropriate</u> to the individual recipient, as well as being <u>sufficient</u> in volume and frequency, and this is how the *halachah* has developed.[1] Moreover, the cases cited in *Sifre*, though on the face of it appearing as luxuries rather than necessities of *ts'dakah*, do adhere to this general rule because of the nature of the recipient.

That the text concentrates on cases largely concerning the עני בן טובים may have merely been a way for the *Tannaim* to emphasise their point. More likely, this reflected a serious practical problem, whereby after the Bar Kochba revolt and Hadrianic Persecutions, many previously wealthy people were swiftly and

---

1. Though Jacobs notes that *Yoreh De'ah* 250:1 does add that 'it would seem right to say that this only applies to the distribution of charity for the community operating as a unit. An individual is not obliged to give a poor man 'sufficient for his need', but the poor man should make his sufferings known to the community. If this is not possible, the individual should give him what he needs if he can afford to do so' (JACOBS, *op. cit.*, p.87). It should also be noted that 'even those supporting the approach based on particularity do not demand responses that are completely beyond the resources of the community (cf BT. Ket. 67b)' (HARTMAN & MARX, *op. cit.*, p.52).

unexpectedly reduced to poverty[1] and became dependent on the goodwill of the community. Parts of the community may, in turn, have resented giving to those who had been previously well off and the Sages may have reacted to this by promoting these interpretations as a means of ensuring that all the community acted properly and continue to give. This seems to indicate strongly that this particular interpretation of Scripture in *Sifre* was being driven by social need, to preserve both the well-being and dignity of this class of poor person.

---

1. 'With the shift from an agricultural society to a largely landless community, the problem of Jewish poverty and starvation assumed a more acute level ... where exile and confiscation of properly were frequent occurrences' (BLOCH, *A Book of Jewish Ethical Concepts: Biblical and Postbiblical*, Ktav Publishing House Inc., p.52).

לֹא תְאַמֵּץ אֶת לְבָבְךָ וְלֹא תִקְפֹּץ אֶת יָדְךָ מֵאָחִיךָ הָאֶבְיוֹן כִּי פָתֹחַ תִּפְתַּח לוֹ דֵּי מַחְסֹרוֹ אֲשֶׁר יֶחְסַר לוֹ

Section 7 - 'without the yoke'

השמר לך הוי זהיר שלא תמנע רחמים שכל המונע רחמים מוקש
לעוברי עבירות ופורק עול שמים מעליו שנאמר בליעל בלי עול
דבר אחר השמר לך בלא תעשה פן בלא תעשה פן יהיה דבר עם לבבך
בליעל לאמר זה שקרוי עבודה זרה נאמר כאן בליעל ונאמר להלן
יצאו אנשים בני בליעל מה בני בליעל האמור להלן עבודה זרה אף
בני בליעל האמור כאן עבודה זרה

('Guard yourself', be careful that you do not withhold mercy, for whoever withholds mercy is compared to transgressors and throws off the yoke of heaven from upon himself as it is said *b'lial* - without the yoke [*b'li ol*]. Another interpretation on 'Guard yourself', 'guard' [implies] a negative command, 'lest' [implies] a negative command. 'Lest there be a thing with your heart [which is] *b'lial*'. This is what is called idolatry [lit. strange worship]. It says here *b'lial* and it says elsewhere 'men went out, the sons of *b'lial*'. Just as 'sons of *b'lial*' it says there [refers to] idolatry, so sons of *b'lial*, [which] it says here [signifies] idolatry.)

The Biblical text makes it quite clear that not to give will mean that you are, or have something within you that is בליעל Most often this is translated as evil, base or wicked - all synonyms designed to convey the negative nature of the דבר (thought or matter) of not giving.[1]

---

1. The usual etymology of this word is that it is a compound of בלי (without) and יעל (worth/profit/advantage), and it can be translated as useless, worthless as well as implying wickedness. See below for other possibilities for its derivation.

The Biblical verse could have used רע (bad/evil) or a similar synonym,[1] but instead it chooses to use this difficult word and associates it with the heart (or as we now read it, the mind - see section 2). The Rabbis clearly perceive this difficulty and this section of the *Midrash* largely centres around their wish to assess the depths of wickedness that the Scriptural use of the word בליעל is trying to convey and why בליעל is used.

The first comment, according to Finklestein's text is, however, on השמר לך (guard yourself). As Hammer notes, Finklestein's text 'is somewhat eclectic'[2] and Finklestein himself notes that this section, הוספה היא זו ולא מעיקר הספרי אעפ"י שנמצאת ברוב הנוסחאות (is an addition, as this is not part of the original *Sifre* text even though it is found in most versions).[3] Given that this section may be a later interpolation we must be wary of deriving too much from it, with respect to the *Tannaim* and their views on *ts'dakah*.

The idea presented is that you are guarding yourself against the withholding of mercy. It's use of הוי זהיר (be careful) reflects an *azharah* (a specific prohibition)[4] establishing that to guard oneself against withholding mercy has the force of a commandment and is not merely sound advice.

Of interest in this passage is the implication that giving *ts'dakah* is an act of mercy and thus not giving is a withholding of such an act. The main *Sifre* text, building on the biblical idea, generally conveys that

---

1. As it does later in connection with one's eye, ורעה עינך באחיך (and your eye be evil against your brother (*D'varim* 15:9).
2. HAMMER, *op. cit.*, p. xiii.
3. FINKELSTEIN, *op. cit.*, p.176. Neusner does not translate this passage in his analytical translation (NEUSNER, *op. cit.*, p.292).
4. JASTROW, *op. cit.*, p.37. It is most often used with reference to 'the explicit prohibition (thou shalt not) in the Bible' (*ibid.*) which perhaps gives an indication of the force of this warning.

ts'dakah is a poor person's right and though emotions have a role to play, it is not really dependent on the pity or compassion of others. Since this section may be a later addition, this reference to רחמים (lit. mercies) could be a reflection of slightly later ideas, such as is found in *Shabbat* 151b where R. Gamliel[1] says, in the name of Rabbi, that,

כל המרחם על הבריות מרחמין עליו מן שמים וכל שאינו מרחם על הבריות אין מרחמין עליו מן השמים

(whoever is merciful to other people, receives mercy from Heaven, and whoever is not merciful to others, receives no mercy from Heaven).

More importantly in this section of our *Sifre* text, we are given the first intepretation of what it might mean to be בליעל. Scripture does not contain vowels, and it is merely the change of one vowel that allows a powerful interpretation, through a creative philology, known as *notarikon*. The pun is more than a mere wordplay; it enables the *Tannaim* to set a measure to the depths of evil of one who is considered בליעל. Such a person is בלי עול (without the yoke [of heaven]) - someone who has abandoned the commandments.

The same interpretation is given first in *Sifre Piska* 93 to *D'varim* 13:14 where בליעל appears for the first time in Scripture,

יצאו אנשים ... בני בליעל בלי עול בני אדם שפרקו עולו של מקום

(men went out ... sons of *b'lial'*, without the yoke, men that have thrown off the yoke of the Omnipresent).[2] A similar explanation is

---

1. Gamliel III, 5th generation *Tanna*, the son of Rabbi, classed by Strack and Stemberger as a half *Tanna*, See STRACK & STEMBERGER, *op. cit.*, p.90.
2. Finkelstein notes a textual difficulty with the section as it appears in *Piska* 93 which seems to be suggesting an alternative derivation for the word, that,

לפי הנוסח הרגיל בני עוול בני אדם וכו' שני הפרושים סותרים מפורש בליעל בניעוול כלו' בני עולה ואי צדק ואחר כך מתבאר בלי עול זה את זה בראשונה

(according to the usual version [of the text it is] *b'ney avel* (sons of injustice), people etc. The two explanations contradict one another. At first it explains *b'ney avel* (sons of injustice), as it says sons of injustice and not righteousness, but after

brought in *Sanhedrin* 111b, though as a comment on the *mishnah* that,

אנשי איר נדחת אין להם חלק לעוה"ב שנאמר יצאו אנשים בני בליעל מקרבך וידיחו את (אנשי) עירם

(the men of a seduced city do not have a portion in the world to come as it says, 'the men, who were the sons of *b'lial*, went out from amongst you and have seduced [the men] of their city').

The version in *Midrash Tannaim* to *D'varim* 15:9 adds further information, that,

שיצאו מתחת כנפי השכינה ופרקו עול שמים מליהם שנ' בלעל בלי עול

(they went out from beneath the wings of the Divine Presence[1] and they threw off the yoke of heaven from upon themselves, as it says *b'lial* without the yoke).

Whereas the biblical text was simply explaining that these men came forth from amongst Israel, the *Tannaim* imply that to go out implies that such a person has spiritually left the community of Israel and thus gone out from the service of God. As a direct result, they have forfeited the protection of God and 'have lost their share in the the future world'.[2]

The *davar acher* that follows (or proceeds in some texts), indicates that both השמר לך (guard yourself) and פן (lest) represent two separate

---

that we find [the exegesis] *b'li ol* (without the yoke ...) (FINKELSTEIN, *op. cit.*, p.154). Rashi (s.v. *Vayikra* 19:15) explains of one who is עול (unjust) that he is שנוי ומשקץ חרם ותועבה (hateful, detested, doomed to destruction and an abomination), Bertinoro reads the word as, בלי יעל 'without ascending' i.e. who will never ascend from the grave to the future world' (*Sanhedrin* 111b, Soncino Hebrew English Ed., note a(12)).

1. A synonym for God's protection and for entering the Jewish community, often applied in Rabbinical literature to *Gerim* (proselytes) who eneter under the wings of the *Sh'chinah* (Divine Presence).
2. *Sanhedrin* 111b, Soncino Hebrew-English Ed. note a(2).

negative commandments. This appears to be a standard interpretation with similar occurring in *Piska'ot* 70 and 81 of *Sifre* but there is no specific statement as to why this should be and what these two commandments actually are. The use of such formulae often accompany a negative prohibition on their own. Since they are used here in conjunction, most likely the *Tannaim* are assuming that there is a doubling of the negative prohibition for emphasis, so that one should realise the seriousness of not giving *ts'dakah*.[1]

It is also possible that the two prohibitions they suggest are echoing the earlier duality of the intention and the deed.[2] השמר (guard) may represent a prohibition against an evil thought, whilst פן (lest) is the prohibition against not physically giving, i.e. in the sense of reading the verse as '<u>guard</u> yourself against the evil thought, (i.e. the דבר עם לבבך בליעל (thing that is with your heart [or mind] [that is] *b'lial*), <u>lest</u> you actually do withhold mercy by not giving'.

Having established the double prohibition, and that the withholder of *ts'dakah* is without the yoke of God, our text moves on to give a new dimension to the meaning of בליעל which appears almost as an extension (or even logical conclusion) to the previous material.[3]

Though many other passages could have been chosen, the Sages have again settled on the first mention of the word in *D'varim* 13:14, this being the most appropriate to Midrashic exegesis since the other appearances are outside of the five books of Moses. This time,

---

1. As Hammer explains '<u>Beware</u> signifies a negative commandment, and the following <u>lest</u> also signifies a negative (thus emphasising the gravity of the command)' (HAMMER, *op. cit.*, p.162). As it happens 'the giving of charity is a mitsvah of special status ... [as it has] a double mandate. It is both a positive commandment and a negative commandment', FREEHOF, S. *New Reform Responsa*, Hebrew Union College Press, 1980, p.176.
2. See section 2 (and also later discussion in section 12).
3. Which may help explain the presence of the interpolation at this point in the *Sifre* text in many versions even though it may not have been in the original redaction.

however, they are drawing on the rest of the verse that explains that the evil men went out and drew others with them,

לאמר נלכה ונעבדה אלוהים אחרים (saying, come and let us serve other gods).[1]

Hence, as Neusner explains, 'the philological analogy imparts to the present usage the meaning established elsewhere',[2] that *b'lial* which it says there [implies] idolatry) and thus when it is used in *D'varim* 15:9 it also means idolatry. Why the Rabbis should choose to make this particular analogy, as opposed to comparing not giving with those בני בליעל[3] (sons of *b'lial*) who in Scripture were guilty of immoral sexual behaviour or murder, is probably no more than them simply

---

1. For example, in *Shoftim* 19:22, the 'sons of *b'lial* are seen terrorising a household, threatening to sexually abuse an old traveller and abusing a concubine in his stead, so that she eventually dies,

   והנה אנשי העיר אנשי בני בליעל נסבו את הבית מתדפקים על הדלת ...
   ויתעללו בה כל הלילה עד בקר

   (and behold men of the city, men, sons of *b'lial*, surrounded the house, beating on the door ... and they abused her all the night until the morning). These men are a part of the tribe of Benjamin, living in *Giv'a* and a cause of civil war since their tribe refuses to deliver them so that ונמיתים ונבערה רעה מישראל (we might put them to death and put away evil from Israel (*Shoftim* 20:13)). According to the Rabbis, three sins that cannot be countenanced, even to save life, and from the above we can see that those who are considered to be בליעל are responsible for promoting these very sins, *avodah zarah* (idolatry), *gilui aryot* (deviant sexual behaviour) and *sh'fichat damim* (murder), giving us an indication of just how serious it is to be considered בליעל. In later references, we learn that those who are בליעל are drunkards (*Sh'muel* 1,1:16), doubters (*ibid.*, 2:12), greedy (*ibid.*, 10:27) and selfish (*ibid.*, 25:25). בליעל is always seen as an internal force, in essence those amongst Israel who are are the 'rotten apples', the 'enemy within', the very antithesis of those who walk in God's paths, one who has abandoned the commandments, of which *ts'dakah* is but one.
2. The link between throwing off the yoke and those who 'went out' has already been shown in *Midrash Tannaim* to *D'varim* 15:9.
3. NEUSNER, *op. cit.*, p.292.

reacting to the first mention of בליעל, which has set the tone for all future interpretations of the word.

A parallel text in *Tosefta P'ah* 4: 20, attributes this interpretation and thus the link to idolatry to R. Y'hoshua ben Korcha.[1] He asks rhetorically, מניין שכל המעלים עיניו מן הצדקה כאילו עובד עבודה זרה (from where [do we learn] that anyone who hides his eyes from [i.e. ignores] *ts'dakah*, it is as if he worshipped idols). The same two verses[2] in combination that we find in *Sifre* then follow.[3]

If the initial section discussed above is part of the original *Sifre* text, one could argue that just as the idolatry of the 'sons of *b'lial*' follows from their going out from the community, so too then the identification of the non-giver as tantamount to being an idolator is a logical extension to one who has thrown off the yoke of heaven - the two exegeses become linked. Moore states that 'the most radical of sins [was] the rejection of God'[4] and for him, the Sages are stressing that 'everyone who refuses charity is put [by the text] in the same category with idolators'.[5] Hirsch suggests a further reason in that 'it is God, in whose Name every demand for help comes to us, and to deny paying sufficient attention to any demand is equivalent to denying God and making money your idol'.[6]

---

1. 3rd generation *Tanna*, see STRACK STEMBERGER, *op. cit.*, p.85.
2. *D'varim* 13:14 and 15: 9.
3. Y'hoshua b. Korcha may also have been drawing on the specific example of Naval, who is called איש הבליעל (a man of *b'lial* (*Sh'muel* I, 25:25)) and elsewhere is decribed as ואיש קשה ורע מעללים (an hard [hearted] man, evil in his deeds (*ibid.*, 25:3). Scripture warns us not to be hard hearted or evil to the poor person, so Naval would clearly be regarded as an uncharitable man.
4. MOORE, *op. cit.*, p.166, note 2. Also, *Sifre* notes elsewhere that, כל המודה בעבודה זרה כופר בכל התורה כולה (whoever acknowledges idolatry is like one who denies the whole Torah (*Sifre Piska* 54)).
5. MOORE, *op. cit.*, p.166.
6. HIRSCH, *op. cit.*, p.273.

Whether this was merely an exaggerative exhortation, or whether the Rabbis were actually suggesting by this exegesis that the sin, and thus the punishment for both idolatry and not giving *ts'dakah* should match,[1] is unclear from Tannaitic material. Certainly the sin of not giving was taken seriously and is cited as the reason behind Hillel's institution of the Prosbul, in that,

שראה את העם שנמנעו מהלוות זה את זה ועברו מה שכתוב בתורה
השמר לך פן יהיה דבר עם לבבך בליעל וגו' עמד והתקין פרוסבול

(when he [Hillel] saw the people that they withheld from loaning to one another, and [thus] they transgressed what is written in the Torah 'guard yourself lest there will be a thing with[in] your heart [that is] *b'lial* etc ... he arose and established [the] *Prosbul*).[2]

This concept of *Prosbul* by which a loan could be paid back after the seventh year when a written agreement was made, was tantamount to an avoidance of Scriptural law and thus an indication of how serious the *Tannaim* took the idea of not lending to the poor.

It is not, however, until the late Amoraic period that we have a practical case showing the link between idolatry and not giving. We read that,

רב פפא הוה סליק בדרגא אישתמיט כרעיה בעי למיפל אמר השתא
כן איחייב מאן דסני לן כמחללי שבתות וכעובדי עבודת כוכבים
א"ל חייא בר רב מדפתי לרב פפא שמא עני בא לידך ולא פרנסתו

---

1. The *Tosefta* renders כאילו (as if) whereas *Sifre* states that שקרוי (this is [actually] called) idolatry. This may suggest that the *Sifre* statement is a more definite, harsher pronouncement of the sin.
2. *Sifre Piska* 113 to *D'varim* 15:3, *Sh'vi'it* 10:3 and *Gittin* 36a. Cohen explains that 'the Scriptural ordinance really deals with an act of charity performed by an Israelite towards a member of his nation in distress and not with a loan contracted in the ordinary course of business. The sociological background of the [Biblical] law [was] a nation of small-holders, each living on the produce of his allotment. When conditions altered and a large section of the population derived a livelihood from commerce, the Biblical regulation became a serious impediment' (COHEN, *op. cit.*, p.xxii). Arguably, therefore, Hillel's reasoning was based as much on a sound understanding of the economic realities as it was on his concern to stop people from transgressing the law.

(Rav Papa was climbing a ladder, his foot slipped and he narrowly escaped falling. He said, if that had happened my enemy [i.e. himself] would have been punished like those who profane Sabbaths and like those who serve idols [lit. service of the stars]. Chiyya b. Rav from Difti said to R. Papa, perhaps a poor person came to appeal to you [lit. to your hand] and you did not support him).[1]

The Biblical punishment for idolators was execution by stoning, 'to which death by a fall was akin'[2] and Chiyya b. Rab from Difti[3] saw this link not merely as a exhortative comparison but almost literally. This penalty, however, was in the hands of God, rather than for an earthly court to impose.[4]

It is clear then from this section of *Sifre* that the *Tannaim* were keen to

---

1. *Bava Batra* 10a.
2. Ibid., Soncino Hebrew-English Ed., note b(7). This is drawing on *Sanhedrin* 45a, which states, ומנין שבסקילה ובדחייה ת"ל סקל יסקל או ירה יירה (and whence do we know that both stoning and hurling down [were employed as means of execution], from the verse 'He shall surely be stoned or surely cast down' (*D'varim* 19:13)).
3. Chiyya b. Rav of Difti (a 5th generation *Amora*) is clearly a keen proponent of this link, reported as bringing forward R. Y'hoshua b.Korcha's teaching both here and again in *K'tubot* 68a.
4. Divine retribution replacing earthly capital punishment appears to have been a reaction to the cessation of the *Sanhedrin*. This meant that 'capital punishment could no longer be decreed by Jewish courts' (*K'tubot* 30a, Soncino Hebrew-English Ed., note c(5)). Instead,
מי שנתחייב סליקה או נופל מן הגגאו חיה דורסתו (he who <u>would have been</u> sentenced to stoning, either falls from a roof or a wild animal tramples him) (*K'tubot* 30b). It is, of course, absolutely unthinkable that anyone was put to death for not giving *ts'dakah* though there were seizures of wealth from those who would not give and were able to do so,
כפינן ליה על כרחיה כי הא דרבא כפייה לרב נתן בר אמי ואפיק מיניה ד' מאה זוזי לצדקה
(if a man is wealthy he may be compelled [to give to charity] even against his wish as was the case with Rava who used compulsion against R. Natan b. Ammi and extracted from him four hundred *zuz* for charity (*K'tubot* 49b)).

reinforce the message of the Scriptural passage by proposing various interpretations of בליעל which indicate the extent to which they viewed failure to give *ts'dakah* as a sin of the highest degree.

This they further emphasised by the doubling of the commandment to guard oneself against behaving in such a manner and to avoid being counted amongst those who are בליעל.

Section 8 - 'seven years for everyone'

קרבה שנת השבע שנת השמטה זו היא שאמר רבי יוסי הגלילי אם שבע שנים לכל אחד ואחד היאך היא קרבה אמור מעתה שבע שנים לכל העולם

('the seventh year (draws] near, the year of *sh'mitta* (release)',[1] 'this is as R. Yose Hag'lili[2] said, if [it means] seven years for each person [individually] how can it '[draw] near', [therefore] it is [the same] seven years for everyone [lit. the whole world]).

D'varim 15:7-11 in its Scriptural context revolves primarily around the difficulties caused by the approach of the seventh year and the negative effect it can have on the giving of loans, as explained in *Midrash Tannaim*,

קרבה שנת השבע שנת השמטה שלא ימנע מהלוות בשביל שלא ישמט ממנו

('the seventh year draws near, the year of *sh'mitta*, that he will not withhold from lending, because he will not release his money).[3] Because of its appropriation by the *Tannaim* to refer to aiding the poor

---

1. מקץ שבע שנים תעשה שמיטה (At the end of seven years you will make a *sh'mitta* (*D'varim* 15:1)). It is not the intention of this section to go into a detailed discussion of the Sabbatical year, which has an entire section of the *Mishnah* plus a *Tosefta* and *Y'rushalmi G'mara* devoted to it, but in short, in the Sabbatical year, 'land must lie fallow and all kinds of labour therein is forbidden; all debts must be remitted; and no trade may be carried on with seventh year produce', (LEHRMAN, S. M, *Introduction to Shebi'ith, Soncino Hebrew-English Ed.*)
2. 2nd generation *Tanna*, see STRACK & STEMBERGER, op. cit., p. 81.
3. Since שביעית משמטת את הלוה (the seventh [year] releases a debt (*Sh'vi'it* 10:1)).

on a more general level,[1] however, the section above is the only part of our *Midrash* that specifically refers to the seventh year.

This passage in *Sifre* repeats verbatim a part of *Piska* 111 where it appears as an essential proof text in a discussion over what is exactly meant by 'seven years' in *D'varim* 15:1. The *Tannaim* pose the question, שבע שנים יכול שבע שנים לכל אחד ואחד ('Seven years'. Is it possible that this [means] seven years for each person [i.e. counting on an individual basis]), and they are particularly concerned as to how this effects loans.

It seems unlikely that the question is raised by the *Tannaim* because they do not know the actual mechanics of the rules concerning loans, since one must assume that it was practiced at least at the time of Hillel, who would not otherwise have gone to all the trouble of instituting the *Prosbul*.[2]

It is likely, though, that the practice of land release had ceased, possibly during the time of the Second Temple and certainly after its destruction in 70 CE.[3] Given that, כל זמן שיש לך שמטה אתה משמט (all the time that you have *sh'mitta* [i.e. the release of land is in force] so you will [also] release [debts]).[4] This was probably not a practical contemporary problem for the *Tannaim* of *Sifre*. Rather, it is possible

---

1. 'In [its] context the reference is to the "year of release" ... but the text was interpreted in Jewish tradition as also indicating a general attitude to the poor' (JACOBS, *op, cit.*, p.79) and thus our 'Midrash extends to gifts and only incidentally touches on loans secured by a pledge' (MOORE, *op. cit.*, p.162).
2. See section 7 for discussion of this institution.
3. 'The Talmud (b. Git. 36a-b) adopts the different line that the biblical law [of release] did not have full legal force in the times of the Second Temple when Hillel lived, since the Jubilee was not in operation' (MACCOBY, *op. cit.*, p.77).
4. *Piska* 111. Hammer gives '[money]' in parenthesis by way of clarification as the Hebrew states 'release' without saying what of (HAMMER, *op. cit.*, p,158). *Emek Han'tsiv* similarly states, כ״ז שיש שמיטת הארץ אתה משמט כספיס (all the time that there is release of the land, you release monies). It is also fairly clear from the Biblical context that this is referring to loans. See PLAUT, G W, *The Torah. A Modern Commentary*, UAHC, 1981, p.1440.

that their concerns are raised rhetorically, so that they may provide an answer that is supported by Scripture, This would ensure the mechanics of the tradition were carefully preserved should it ever be in force again.

The problem over what constitutes 'seven years' exists because there are two possible answers, depending on whether one draws on the release of land or the release of slaves as a model for comparison,

הרי אתה דן חייב שבע שנים בשמטה וחייב שבע שנים במלוה מה שבע שנים האמור בשמטה שבע שנים לכל העולם אף שבע שנים האמור במלוה שבע שנים לכל העולם או כלך לדרך זו חייב שבע שנים בעבד עברי וחייב שבע שנים מה שבע שנים האמור בעבד עברי שבע שנים לכל אחד ואחד אף שבע שנים האמור במלוה שבע שנים לכל אחד ואחד

(Behold you may reason thus; one is obligated [after] seven years concerning *sh'mitta* [of land][1] and obligated [after] seven years concerning loans. Just as [the] seven years [that are] spoken of concerning *sh'mitta* of land are [common][2] for everyone, so [the] seven years [that are] spoken of concerning loans [are] seven years for everyone. Or perhaps [your reasoning may go] this way, [since you are] obligated [after] seven years concerning the Israelite slave[3] and obligated [after] seven years concerning loans. Just as [the] seven years [that are] spoken of concerning the Israelite slave [varies] from individual to individual, so [the] seven years [that are] spoken of concerning loans [are] seven years for each individual).[4]

---

1. *Emek Han'tsiv* clarifies here that, חייב שבע שנים בשמיטה שמיטת הארץ (bound seven years concerning *sh'mitta*, [refers to) the *sh'mitta* of land).
2. Hammer renders 'a uniform counting' (HAMMER, *op. cit.*, p.158).
3. כי ימכר לך אחיך העברי או העריה ועבדך שש שנים ובשנה השביעית תשלחנו חפשי (if your Israclite brother sells himself to ([and this applies also to] an Israelite woman [who is a slave]), he will serve you six years, and in the seventh year, you will set him free (*D'varim* 15: 12)).
4. *Piska* 111 to *D'varim* 15:1.

Some lengthy discussion then follows on each case to determine which better resembles that of lending.. Reference is also made to their relation to the Jubilee year and their operation inside or outside the land. The proof finally given which relates the case of loans to that of the release of land is that,

תלמוד לומר שבע שנים שבע שנים לגזרה שוה מה שבע שנים האמור בשמטה שבע שנים לכל העולם אף שבע שנים האמור במלוה שבע שנים לכל העולם

(Scripture says 'seven years' [in one place and] 'seven years' in another place] [leading] to a *g'zerah shavah* [therefore] just as [the] seven years [that are] spoken of concerning *sh'mitta* [of land are] seven years [which] are [common] for everyone, so [the] seven years [that are] spoken of concerning loans are for everyone).[1]

Utilising the hermeneutical technique of *g'zerah shavah*, the link is established beyond that of mere logic, as it is Torah itself which informs the *Tannaim* of the correct solution.[2]

However for the argument to be complete, the *Tannaim* needs to prove that it is indeed the case that the release of land has a common seven year period (and thus by extension so does the release of loans). It is the opinion of R. Yose Hag'lili, quoted above, that allows this by asking logically how else it could approach if it were not a commonly shared event happening at a specific time.

The argument brought by the *Tannaim* in Piska 111 is convoluted, and possibly suspect. The *g'zerah shavah* they propose is, on one hand, *D'varim* 15:1 which does give שבע שנים (seven years) and is the only reference concerning loans to do so.[3]

---

1. Piska 111.
2. 'Logic alone could lead to incorrect halachic conclusions, and thus requires the specific limitations and expansions which Scripture specifies' (HAMMER, *op. cit.*, p.12).
3. *D'varim* 15:9 gives שנת השבע (the seventh year). Hammer seems to suggest the

With reference to the standard Sabbatical year for land and שבע שנים[1] the only candidate for the link appears to be *Vayikra* 25: 8, which gives, וספרת לך שבע שבתות שנים שבע שנים שבע פעמים (and you will count for yourself seven Sabbatical years, <u>seven years</u>, seven times). Though the reference is to the release of land, its Biblical context centres around the fifty year Jubilee and not the normal Sabbatical year of seven years. The period of seven years is, in reality, not common to both at all, weakening their argument,

Moreover, the *Tannaim* could quite easily have been able to deduce that the seventh year for loans is the same for everyone purely from *D'varim* 15:9, קרבה שנת השבע (the seventh year <u>draws near</u>) since it refers to loans in its original context and thus they had no need to link it to the release of land at all.

Clearly in *Piska* 111 the *Tannaim* felt the need to demonstrate a link between these two releases. Perhaps this is more to establish that as long as the release of land was held in abeyance the release of debts would similarly not be in operation, than to demonstrate the way the loan release operated with regard to the passing of time. The apparent re-appearance of this interpretation within *Piska* 117, is quite logical since R. Yose Haglili's opinion was based on *D'varim* 15:9, and, as we have seen above, it is quite able to stand alone as a proof.[2]

---

link is between 15:1 and 15:9, but both are about loan debts and a link would therefore not establish anything. (HAMMER, *op. cit.*, p.437).

1. For example *Sh'mot* 23:10 which gives השביעית (the seventh [year]) and *Vayikra* 25:4 which reads ובשנה השביעית (and in the seventh year). These however speak of the release of land in the context of allowing it to lie fallow rather than releasing it to previous ownership, and so would not have resembled the case of remission of debts as much as the release of the land in the Jubilee would have.
2. Indeed it may have stood alone originally and been employed by the *Tannaim* in *Piska* 111 as part of their discussions subsequently.

Section 9 - 'quicker to exact retribution'

ורעה עינך באחיך האביון ולא תתן לו וקרא עליך אל ה׳ יכול מצוה
לקרות תלמוד לומר וקרא יכול מצוה לקרות תלמוד לומר ולא יקרא
עליך יכול אם קרא עליך יהיה בך חטא ואם לאו לא יהיה בך תלמוד
לומר והיה בך חטא מכל מקום עם כן למה נאמר וקרא עליך אל ה׳
ממהר אני ליפרע על יד קורא יותר ממי שאינו קורא

('And your eye be evil against your brother the needy person and you do not give to him and he calls out against you to God'. Is it possible [that] it is a commandment not to call out? Scripture says 'and he calls out'. Is it possible [that] it is a commandment to call out? Scripture says 'and he will not call out against you'. Is it possible [that] if he calls out against you there will be within you sin, but [that] if he does not [call out against you] there will not be sin? Scripture says 'and there will be within you sin' - in each case. If so, why does it say 'and he calls out against you to God'? [Because] I [God] will be quicker to exact retribution on behalf of one who calls out, more than one who does not call out).

Before examining the comment on the verse in detail, it is worth noting the *Tannaim* in *Sifre* make no comment on ורעה עיניך (and your eye be evil),[1] the only section of the text where this is the case. Given that we have already seen how your mind, heart and your hand can be set against the poor, one might have expected a comment as to what it means for one's eye to be evil. Perhaps it was accepted as a standard phrase, still in common usage and thus not worthy of further comment,

---

1. Neusner renders 'so that you are <u>mean</u> to your needy kinsman', (NEUSNER *op. cit.*, p.293), which does not really convey the full meaning.

meaning to avert your eyes or simply to ignore. This may be seen in the preamble to the *baraita* on *b'lial* that we have already discussed, and which read,

אמ' ר' יהושע בן קרחה ... שכל המעלים עיניו מן הצדקה עובד ע"ז

(R. Y'hoshua ben Korcha said ... that all who hide their eyes from [the opportunity of giving] *ts'dakah*, it is as if they practised idolatry).[1]

The concerns of the *Tannaim* centre instead initially around whether there is a commandment implied in the text and if so, what it might be. The text utilises a standard form, *yakol ... talmud lomar'*, which Hammer renders as 'you might think ... hence' and which he states 'appears frequently [in *Sifre*] and almost without exception introduces a proposition which is to be negated: this is what we might have thought, but Scripture specifically indicates otherwise'.[2] Indeed, this is the case here.

Hammer further suggests that 'since one might think that this continues the list of what should not be done, [i.e. in this verse, one's eye should not be evil and one shouldn't with-hold from him] we are told specifically that the needy person is permitted, perhaps encouraged, to cry out when you do him an injustice'.[3] Hence, according to Hammer, the *Tannaim* may have concluded that you also should not call out. Scripture says specifically וקרא (and he calls out) and therefore they hold it to be a separate element of the verse, not part of a list of prohibitions.

It is worth noting that though this first section and the question

---

1. *Tosefta Pe'ah* 4: 20 and *Bava Batra* 10a. See section 7 for discussion. Eisenstein, drawing on the *Shulchan Aruch*, notes that,
   ואחד מעשרה מהרויח היא מדה בינונית פחות מכאן עין רעה ([to give] one tenth from your income, this is a middling measure, less than this [your) eye is evil [to the poor]) (EISENSTEIN, אוצר דינים ומנהגים, *A digest of Jewish Laws and Customs*, Israel, 1975, p.346).
2. HAMMER, *op. cit.*, p.12.
3. *Ibid.*, p.439.

יכול מצוה לקרות תלמוד לומר וקרא (is it possible that it is a commandment not to call? Scripture says 'and he calls') appears in many of the *Sifre* manuscripts,[1] it is omitted from the London manuscript and several printed sources. These versions begin the exegesis more logically, (since וקרא (and he calls) is framed as a positive statement), and ask the question יכול מצוה לקרות (is it possible that it is a commandment to call out?).

The answer provided, תלמוד לומר ולא יקרא עליך (Scripture says 'and he will not call against you' draws upon *D'varim* 24:15 where there is a similar phrasing concerning a sin being committed, though in this instance with regard to withholding a person's wage till the next day.[2] Since, on that occasion, Scripture states ולא יקרא (and he will not call out), the *Tannaim* conclude that no inference can be drawn either way. If it were a positive commandment to call in *D'varim* 15.9, then how could there be a commandment not to call, later in the *Torah*?

This comparison of *D'varim* 15:9 with *D'varim* 24:15 has also provided an answer to the other element of the question posed by the *Tannaim* - i.e. whether sin would still be accounted against a person who was not called out against?

A literal reading of *D'varim* 15:9, might suggest the cause and effect is וקרא עליך ... והיה בך חטא (and he calls against you ... and [therefore] there will be in you sin). This would imply that the sin is

---

1. See FINKELSTEIN, *op. cit.*, p.176, note 9. The GR"A also leaves it out of his emendations.
2. ביומו תתן שכרו ולא תבוא עליו השמש כי עני הוא ואליו הוא נשא את נפשו ולא יקרא עליך אל ה' והיה בך חטא
(on that day you will give [him] his wage and the sun will go down upon him [before he receives it] for he is poor and relies [lit, sets his soul] upon it and [then] he will not call out against you to the Lord that there will be within you sin (*D'varim* 24:15)).

somehow related to the act of calling rather than to the admonition ולא תתן (and you do not give).

In order to counter this, the *Tannaim* read *D'varim* 24:15 somewhat atomistically. Instead of reading, ולא יקרא עליך אל ה׳ והיה בך חטא (and [then] he will not call out against you to the Lord that there will be within you sin) they separate the two elements such that ולא יקרא עליך (and he will not call out against you) but nonetheless והיה בך חטא (and there will [still] be within you sin).

Having established, by this, that you will have sinned <u>even when he doesn't call out</u> the *Tannaim* are able to assert that the outcome is the same בכל מקום (in each case [lit. place and implying the two verses]).[1]

It is now that one sees where the *Tannaim* are heading, and what is really troubling them. For, if it does not signify a commandment and whether one calls or not it is still accounted as a sin, (and certainly there is no consideration given by the *Tannaim* that God, who is Omnipresent would need to be told that a sin is being committed), then, עם כן למה נאמר וקרא עליך אל ה׳ (if so, why does it say 'and he calls out against you to God'?) There must be a reason since such a major redundancy in the Biblical text could not be tolerated.

Their conclusion is that the cause and effect is related not to the sin but to the punishment. God acts <u>more speedily</u> to punish those who are called out against. However, this idea is nowhere implied by the text. It is apparently a purely logical deduction by the *Tannaim* and may be based on assumption that if one is prepared to call out against another to God because of his maltreatment then it must have had a deeper

---

1. *Emek Han'tsiv* proposes a different understanding in that the *Tannaim* saw והיה not as a *vav* consecutive meaning 'and there will be' but as 'and there was', i.e. והיה משמע שהיה כבר קודם שקרא (*v'hayah* - teaches that it [sin] was already there <u>before</u> he called).

effect[1] on him than for one who does not call out.

Certainly God is held to give preferential treatment to the poor generally, for elsewhere in *Sifre* we learn that,

ואם איש אני הוא אין לי אלא עני עשיר מנין תלמוד לומר ואם איש אם כן למה נאמר עני ממהר אני ליפרע על ידי עני יותר מן העשיר

('and if he be a poor man' (*D'varim* 24:12), I only know this of a poor man, from where [do we learn it applies to] a rich man, [because] Scripture says 'and if a man' [implying any man]. If so, why does it say poor? Because I exact retribution on behalf of the poor man more quickly than the rich man).[2] Again, in the case of withholding wages,

אין לי אלא עני ואביון מנין לרבות כל אדם תלמוד לומר לא תעשוק מכל מקום אם כן למה נאמר עני ואביון ממהר אני ליפרע על ידי עני ואביון יותר מכל אדם

(I only know this [that one doesn't oppress by with-holding the wages] of the poor and needy. From where [do we learn it applies] to all men, Scripture says 'Do not oppress' in both cases. If so, why does Scripture say 'poor and needy'? (*D'varim* 24:14) Because I punish on behalf of the poor and needy more than all [other] men).[3] In both cases, the *Tannaim* have shown the commandment to apply equally to all men, not just the poor, so the references to the poor are, in their eyes, similarly redundant and requiring explanation.

The formula of the explanation is standard in all three cases, that of למה נאמר (why does it say), with the answer ממהר אני ליפרע על ידי (I [God] am quicker to exact retribution on behalf of). This clearly represents one of many conventions the *Tannaim* employed to deal with potential redundancy. As to why this might be, Hammer notes that

---

1. For example, Ben Sira states that 'when he begs for alms do not look the other way and so give him reason to curse you, for if he curse you in his bitterness his Maker will listen to his prayers' (Eccleslasticus 4:5, *op. cit.*, p.163).
2. *Piska* 277 to *D'varim* 24:12.
3. *Piska* 278 to *D'varim* 24:14.

'the cause of the poor is more urgent in the sight of God'[1] since 'the poor have no-one to turn to but God'.[2]

It is also worth considering what the *Tannaim* meant by God being quicker to punish. The root פרע also implies the collection of a debt or exacting retribution[3] and in the *Targumim* the word used to translate the Hebrew חטא (sin) in this instance and in many others, is חובא which also implies a debt, perhaps an indebtedness to God.[4] In Rabbinic theology, as we have seen in our examination of the concept of *galgal*, (the wheel),[5] retribution for sin does not need to be instantaneous. God will call the sinner to account sooner or later'. Perhaps in the case of one who is called out against, we learn that it is <u>sooner</u> rather than later.

Finally, on the theme of retribution, *Midrash Tannaim* offers an additional insight into והיה בך חטא (and it will be within you a sin), explaining that,

שלא תאמר בממון חטאתי בממון נפרעין ממני ת״ל והיה בך חטא
ממך נפרעין אין נפרעין ממונך

(that you will not say with money I sinned, with money retribution will

---

1. HAMMER, *op. cit.*, p.479, note 2 to *Piska* 277. *Ibid.*, p. 480, note 4 to *Piska* 277.
2. A similar explanation is given in the *M'chilta de R. Yishma'el* to *Sh'mot* 22:21 discussing the regular recipients of *ts'dakah*, the widow and orphan,

כי אם צעוק יצעק אלי שמוע אשמע צעקתו כל זמן שהוא צועק אני שומע
ואם אינו צועק איני שומע הא מה ת״ל שמוע אשמע אלא ממהר אני לפרא
ע״י שהוא צועק יותר ממי שאינו צועק

('or if he surely cry out to me, I [God] will surely hear', each time that he cries I hear and if he does not cry I won't hear? Surely not, what [does Scripture mean by] 'I will surely hear'? Rather [it implies] that I [God] will be quicker to exact retribution on behalf of one that cries out, than one who does not cry out. *Ben Sira* similarly states that, 'He [God] has no favourites at the poor man's expense but listens to his prayer when he is wronged' (Ecclesiasticus 21:5, *op. cit.*, p.218) and that 'the Lord listens to the poor man's appeal and his verdict follows without delay' (*ibid.*, 21:5, p.192).
3. JASTROW, *op. cit.*, p.1235,
4. *Targum Onkelos* to *D'varim* 15.9. See JASTROW, *op. cit.*, p.429.
5. See section 3.

be exacted from me. Scripture says 'and it will be within you a sin', [meaning] from you retribution will be exacted, not retribution from your money). It further explains that this personal retribution is that,

ומידבק בעשרים וארבע קללות ... יהיו ימיו מעטים יהיו בניו יתומים ...

([there] will cling to him twenty four curses ... [for example] his days will be shorter, his sons will be orphans [etc] ...).[1]

Such an understanding of the retribution implied by the verse does conflict with the measured retribution of *galgal* which revolved around monetary punishment,[2] and indeed against the whole concept of *middah k'neged middah*. This statement may therefore have represented a different school of Tannaitic thought which argued for even harsher punishment of those whose 'eye was evil' and who therefore do not give, and perhaps is another indication of how seriously they viewed the failure to give *ts'dakah*.

---

1. *Midrash Tannaim* to *D'varim* 15:9. The text continues to list the twenty four curses.
2. i.e. that they or their descendents will be reduced to poverty. See section 3.

Section 10 - 'you will surely give'

מנין שאם נתת פעם אחת אתה נותן לו אפי' ק' פעמים ת"ל נתון תתן

(From where [do we learn that) if you gave to him once, you give to him even a hundred times? Scripture says, 'you will surely give'.)

See section 4 for full discussion of this element of the text.

Section 11 - 'the Chamber of Secrets'

לו בינך לבינו מכאן אמרו לשכת חשאים היתה בירושלם

('To him' [implying just] between you and him. From this[1] they said there was a Chamber of Secrets[2] in Jerusalem.)

Once again[3] the presence of לו (to him) in the verse is found to be superfluous.[4] This presents a further opportunity for the *Tannaim* to read into the text a lesson in how to give *ts'dakah*, which again stresses the need to avoid shaming the recipient.

Hammer translates מיכן אמרו as '<u>that is why</u> [there was a chamber of secrets in Jerusalem]'[5] and to his mind the *Tannaim* have brought the example to give the existence of the chamber a Scriptural support. This is quite possible, since the Mishnaic reference supplies none.[6]

A literal translation of בינך לבינו (between you and between him),[7]

---

1. This may not convey the full sense here, see below for discussion.
2. Or perhaps 'secret givers', referring to the people who gave in secret rather than the deeds which were secret. Montefiore and Loewe give 'Vestry of Secret Ones' (MONTEFIORE & LOEWE, *op. cit.*, p.420).
3. See section 6.
4. ממלת לו המיותר ([derived] from the superfluous 'to him'), *Toldot Adam*.
5. HAMMER, *op. cit.*, p.163.
6. 'Although an independent work ... in the final redaction [*Sifre*] is concerned to support the Mishnah by citing the scriptural basis for the mishnaic ruling wherever possible', (*ibid.*, p.7).
7. Hammer's translation 'it is (an obligation) between you and him' (*ibid.*, p.163) might be taken to imply this. Neusner's rendering '[keep the matter] between him and you' (NEUSNER, *op. cit.*, p.293) seems better, but still may not convey the full

might be thought to indicate a personal transaction between the parties, which they conduct in private. However, the illustration they select and thereby posit as method to be preferred, is far from personal.[1] Instead they refer to one particular way that *ts'dakah* was given in Temple times not merely where 'the gift to the poor must be made privately with no-one else present',[2] but where neither party would even be aware of whom the other was, since they do not actually meet. If the *Tannaim* are positing a cause and effect between their Scriptural proof and the existence of the chamber, however anachronistic that might be,[3] we could understand בינך לבינו as implying 'between you, <u>where you know only that you gave</u> and between him, <u>where he knows only that he took</u>, with no other involved'.[4]

מיכן אמרו in *Sifre*, appears to refer to a tradition preserved in *Sh'kalim* 5:6 where we read,

שני לשכות היו במקדש אחת לשכת חשאים ... יראי חטא נותנים לתוכה בחשאי עניים בני טובים מתפרנסים בתוכה בחשאי

([that] there were two chambers in the Temple, one [was] the Chamber of Secrets ... fearers of sin gave into it in secret and poor people of

---

meaning.
1. The commentary *Minchat B'chorim* to *Tosefta Sh'kalim* 2:16 explains the process,

   לשכת חשאים ששם זורקין מעות לצדקה בחשאי כדי לפרנס בהם עניים בני טובים המתביישים לקבל בפרהסיא מן הנותן

   ([the Chamber of Secrets - where [they] throw in monies for *ts'dakah* in secret, in order to support thereby, the poor people of good family who are ashamed to receive in public from the giver).
2. MOORE, *op. cit.*, p.167.
3. Though use of מנין אמרו may imply a very old tradition that was current at Temple times.
4. This is, of course, Rambam's penultimate level of *ts'dakah* giving,

   פחות מזה הנותן צדקה לעניים ולא ידע למי נתן ולא ידע העני ממי לקח

   (less than this [i.e. the highest degree] is one who gives *ts'dakah* to the poor and does not know to whom he gives and the poor does not know from whom he takes) and Rambam also brings the Chamber of Secrets as an example of this (*Mishneh Torah: Hilchot Mat'not Aniyim* 10:8). See Appendix 1.

good family supported themselves from it in secret).

Examining this text in detail, it seems that this method of giving *ts'dakah*, is an ideal, restricted to an elite, and not a general practice.

Concerning the giver, we are informed that these were יראי חטא (fearers of sin). The Soncino *Talmud* editors note that these were 'pious persons who sought to avoid publicity for their deeds of charity',[1] whilst Moore suggests these were 'particularly scrupulous persons',[2] and Urbach explains by reference to various sources that the 'designation 'sin fearing' was specifically applied to men who in the same measure as they were careful to avoid trangressions were scrupulous in the observance of the commandments with devotion and love'.[3]

The Scriptural text tells us that ולא תתן לו ... והיה בך חטא (and you do not give to him ... there will be in you sin),[4] so 'sin fearers' would have good reason to worry. Moreover, even if they did give, they would also need to consider the manner in which they did so, which as we know was held to be just as important,[5] for example,

ר' אלאזר המועדי אומר ... [ו]המלבין פני חברו ברבים ... אע"פ
שיש בידו תורה ומעשים טובים אין לו חלק לעולם הבא

---

1. *Sh'kalim* 5:6, *Soncino Hebrew-English Ed.*
2. MOORE, *op. cit.*, p.167.
3. URBACH, *op. cit.*, p.416 Maccoby suggests that they 'were regarded as specially virtuous persons in that they exercised no personal choice over the recipients of their generosity, made no discriminations, and asked for no gratitude or public acknowledgement', (MACCOBY, *op. cit.*, p.86). *Shabbat* 31b speaks of an *Amora*, R. Ya'akov b. Acha who was respected by two of his colleagues more because he was a 'sin-fearer' than because he was a learned man.
4. *D'varim* 15:9.
5. See discussion on *bushah* (shame) in section 4.

(R. Eleazar of Modi'in[1] says ... if a man shames his fellow[2] in public ... even if he has to his credit [knowledge of] Torah and good deeds, he will have no portion in the world to come).[3] And finally, we also learn that for, נותנה ואינו יודע למי נותנה נוטלה ואינו יודע ממי נוטלה (one who gives and does not know to whom he gives and one who takes and does not know from whom he takes), as was the case with the Chamber of Secrets, זו היא שמצילתו ממיתה משונה (this is [the kind of *ts'dakah*] that saves one from an unnatural death).[4]

'Sin fearers', if we accept the various definitions given above, would have taken these lessons to heart to ensure that not only did they give to avoid sin but gave in such a way that did not shame others. Thus they would minimise their fear that their giving would not be wholly acceptable.

Further, this mode of giving was originally only operative in the Temple in Jerusalem, so we are referring to people who make the special and possibly dangerous[5] pilgrimage to the Temple to give in

---

1. 2nd generation *Tanna*, see STRACK & STEMBERGER, *op. cit.*, p.78.
2. Lit. 'whitens his fellow's face'. The Soncino notes that one source reads המאדים 'he who causes etc. ... to redden'. המלבין is explained in B.M 58b [as] 'the blush subsides and whiteness takes its place'. (*Avot* 9a, *Soncino Hebrew-English Ed.*, note d(5)).
3. *Avot* 3:11.
4. *Bava Batra* 10a/b, based on the idea that וצדקה תציל ממות (and *ts'dakah* ['righteousness' in context, but taken by the Rabbis to imply charitable deeds] delivers [one] from death) (*Mishley* 10:2).
5. Assuming we accept a) the accuracy of the text and b) an historical basis for *Tosefta Ta'anit* 4:7-8 that,
שבעה שהושיבו מלכי יון פרתסאות על הדרכים שלא לעלות לירושלים כדרך ירבעם
(the Greek kings posted guards along the roads so as to prevent (pilgrims) from going up to Jerusalem, just as Jeroboam had done), nevertheless, (all who were proper and feared sin - in that same generation carried the first fruits). See URBACH, *op. cit.*, p.870, note 88 for discussion.

this manner. All this would seem to indicate a very special type of person, who is operating far above the normal requirement for the *mitsvah*.

Sh'kalim 5:6 also indicates that the recipients are a special case. We are already familiar with the עני בן טוים (poor of good family),[1] and that this chamber was specifically designed to preserve such a person's dignity is understandable, given that they would have experienced the most shame from a public transaction.[2]

Though this mode of giving *ts'dakah* was originally restricted to a transaction between the very pious and the previously wealthy, and indeed, only in Jerusalem, there does appear to have been some attempt at widening the scope of this method.

A parallel text in *Midrash Tannaim* differs from that of *Sh'kalim* explaining of this chamber,

שהיו הצדיקים נותנין בה (בחשאי) ועניים בני טובים מתפרנסין ממנה בחשאי

(that the <u>righteous</u> give into in secret and the poor people of good family support themselves from it in secret)[3] The givers are now defined as 'righteous' and thus as Urbach argues, could be any person who gives to charity and not just the elite few.[4] Moreover, it is a more

---

1. See sections 3 and 6.
2. As Maccoby asserts 'this was the only form of charity in which there was complete secrecy ... other forms of charity were less secret; the poor taking the *pe'ah* for example were publicly identified as poor by resorting to fields for that purpose and even those who took from the poor-box (quppah) had to make themselves known to the three people who acted as distributors. Such identification would be particularly hard on 'people of good family' ... [who] would be too embarrassed because of their respectable antecendents to apply to the normal sources of charity, and might therefore be in danger of starvation' (MACCOBY, *op. cit.*, p.86).
3. *Midrash Tannaim* to *D'varim* 15:10.
4. Urbach suggests that 'the term saddiq ... serves as a designation for those who do God's will' and that 'the name saddiq is ... given to one who gives charity [sedaqa]', since 'in fulfiling [sedaqa] a man imitates the deeds of his Creator and merits to be called by His name li.e. saddiq]' (URBACH, *op. cit.*, p.484).

positive epithet than the somewhat negative 'sin fearers'.

More concrete evidence of attempts to make this method of giving more widespread can be seen in *Tosefta Sh'kalim* 2:16, which explains,

תניא כשם שהיו לשכת חשאים בירושלים כך היה בכל עיר ועיר מפני שעניים בני טובים מתפרנסין מתוכה בחשאי

(it is taught that just as there was a Chamber of Secrets in Jerusalem so there was [a similar institution] in every city for the poor people of good family to support themselves from it in secret).

There does not, however, seem to be any text that suggests a widening to include recipients other than the previously wealthy. Presumably the *Tannaim* felt that these other poor were catered for within the normal, yet public, system of *tamchui*, *kuppah* etc, for having never been in a position other than poverty, they would not be ashamed by it.

It is worth noting, however, that because of the inherent secrecy of the method, there was no way to 'apply a test to the recipient'[1] and though it is firmly positioned for use by the בני טובים, others could have used it as well.

In summary, the principle being established here as an ideal is for a mode of giving where the donor is anonymous and the poor person is not identified to anyone, even the giver. The method referred to by *Sifre*, quoting from *Sh'kalim* appears somewhat restricted as regards both the giver and recipient, though may have been used more widely than the base text suggests, as time progressed.

---

1. MACCOBY, *op. cit.*, p.86.

It should also be noted, before closing, that one means that was recommended by the *Tannaim* comes close to this ideal and was clearly very much more common, which was, ליתיב לארנקי של צדקה (to give to the *ts'dakah* box)[1] which is as just as easy for us to do today.

---

1. *Bava Batra* 10b. This method clearly can preserve the anonymity of the donor from the recipient and the donor does not know to whom they give. Rambam agrees that, קרוב זה הנותן לקופה של צדקה (close to this [Chamber of Secrets in efficacy] is one who gives to the *ts'dakah* fund' (*Mishneh Torah: Hilchot Mat'not Aniyim* 10:8)). Its failure to reach the high standard of the Chamber of Secrets, is that there would need to be an administrator of the poor box, to whom the poor would have to identify themselves and perhaps be embarrassed. Nonetheless this method, is still seen to 'deliver from death', as long as the administrator is trustworthy. Interestingly, an opposing view to that of the giver not knowing whom the recipient is, is brought by Ben Sira who states, 'if you do a good deed, make sure to whom you are doing it; then you will have credit for your kindness' . (Ecclesiasticus 12:1, *op. cit.*, p.177),

Section 12 - 'a reward for the saying - a reward for the deed'

כי בגלל הדבר הזה אם אמר ליתן ונתן נותנים לו שכר אמירה ושכר מעשה אמר ליתן ולא הספיק בידו ליתן נותנים לו שכר אמירה כשכר מעשה לא אמר ליתן אבל אמר לאחרים תנו נותנים לו שכר על כך שנאמר כי בגלל הדבר הזה לא אמר ליתן ולא אמר לאחרים תנו אבל נוח לו בדברים טובים מנין שנותנים לו שכר על כך תלמוד לומר כי בגלל הדבר הזה יברכך ה' אלקיך בכל מעשיך

('For because of this thing', if one said [he intended] to give and gave, we give him a reward [for the] saying and a reward [for the] deed. [If] one said [he intended] to give and it was not sufficiently in his power [to do so], we give to him a reward [for the saying] as the reward [for the) deed. [If] one did not say [he intended] to give but said to others "Give!", we give to him a reward for this, as it says 'for because of this thing'. [If] one did not say [he intended] to give and did not say to others - "Give!", but put him [i.e. the needy person] at ease with good words, from where [do we learn] that we give to him a reward for this? Scripture says 'for because of this thing, the Lord your God will bless you in all your deeds ...'.)

There is a clear echo here of the ideas of <u>intention</u> and <u>action</u> that has already covered by the Rabbis' interpretation of the two elements to giving symbolised by the לב (mind = intention) and the יד (hand = deed).[1] Also, the two negative commands[2] are here countered with two

---

1. See section 2.
2. See section 7.

rewards for carrying out God's will, the שכר אמירה (reward for the saying) and שכר מעשה (reward for the deed).

This dualism of reward may have sprung from the full verse in *D'varim* which appears to specify the reward in two parts, in that, יברכך ה' אלקיך בכל מעשיך ובכל משלח ידך, (The Lord your God will bless you in all your deeds and in all you put your hands to [lit. the sending of your hands]).[1] Neusner translates this as 'in all your <u>efforts</u> and in all your <u>undertakings</u>',[2] apparently in accordance with the ideas of intention leading to action.[3]

Regardless of what may have started the chain of logic for the Sages, the structure that they then weave is dependent on the many meanings of the single word דבר (a word, utterance, command, matter, thing, affair, object, occurrence).[4]

In its Biblical context, דבר here is clearly referring to an action, i.e. the giving of *ts'dakah*. Even without the subsequent amplification of the *Sifre* text there is evidently a direct cause and effect here; because you gave *ts'dakah*, you will receive a reward, the שכר מעשה (reward for the deed).

In terms of the Scriptural verse, the likelihood is that what the Rabbis saw as implying a two-fold reward was nothing more than a parallelism

---

1. *D'varim* 15:10. That a parallel text in the normally apodictic *Tosefta* (i.e. *Tosefta Pe'ah* 4:17) also makes reference to the Scriptural verse might suggest that this is a development from the verse rather than a reading back into it of an agreed practice.
2. NEUSNER, *op. cit.*, p.294.
3. It may be that the *Tannaim* are deliberately reading מעשיך (your deeds) here not as related to the מעשה (deed), but rather as the *Hiphil* form of the verb עשה (to do), rendering as מעשיך 'your causing to happen', i.e. your intention. However, it must be noted that since the word מעשה does generally imply an action, Neusner's translation as 'efforts' may not be appropriate.
4. *Ibid.*, p.278.

of the text which referred simply to success in agricultural endeavours.[1]

Elsewhere in *Sifre*, we read a comment on *D'varim* 14:29 which explains,

למען יברכך ה' אלקיך בכל מעשה ידך קבע לו הכתוב ברכה בשליחות יד על הארץ אשר אתה בא לרשתה בשכך שתבא תירש

('so that the Lord will bless you in all the deeds of your hands'. Scripture has fixed for him a blessing in his efforts [lit. sendings of the hand] upon the land which you come there to possess it, as a reward for going in, you will possess it).[2] We thus understand the reward as being both the working of the land and the land of Israel itself. Similarly, it may be this reward that is being thought of in *D'varim* 15:10.

The initial comment on this verse is to a large extent the *p'shat* (plain meaning).[3] After this, the true exegesis begins, for in order to convey further aspects to the performance of the *mitsvah*, the Sages have also taken דבר in it meaning of 'words' or even 'thought', where it is signalling one's intention to do something. Hence one also receives a שכר אמירה (reward for the speaking).

It is unclear whether this refers only to stating one's intention out loud for all to hear, or whether it applies also to a promise to give that is just a private thought or intention.

Tosafta Pe'ah 1:4 reports that,

מחשבה טובה המקום ברוך הוא מצפה למעשה (a good thought, God (lit. The Place), Blessed be He, joins it[4] to the deed (i.e. makes it

---

1. Given the Israelites' overwhelmingly rural lifestyle in Biblical times.
2. *Sifre Piska* 263.
3. Though arguably the plainest meaning is delivered by *Midrash Tannaim* to *D'varim* 15:10, which states, ד"א כי בגלל הדבר הזה יב' בגלל שייטיב לך (Another interpretation [of] 'for because of this thing [the Lord your God] will bless you', because he will cause it to go well for you).
4. Or perhaps 'hardens it to the deed'.

happen)). Here the intention is not voiced but nonetheless does still receive the reward for the thought, by it becoming reality.

Given the use of אמר in *Sifre*, rather than חשב (think), it is possible that the additional reward is being restricted here to promises that are actually verbalised in public before the deed.[1] Bloch notes that 'a pledge of charity made in public must be speedily redeemed',[2] and reports that 'according to Rabbi Yochanan b. Zakkai (1st cent.) the failure to redeem public pledges was one of the causes of the downfall of Jerusalem'.[3] Clearly making such announcements openly in the community was a common practice in those days.

As Neusner suggests, since we have begun a chain of logic, 'the program at hand lays out all the possibilities of the case'.[4] The first extension of the case concerns one who has promised to give ולא הפסיק בידו (but it is not sufficiently in his power [to do so]) for some reason, possibly a change in circumstances, but clearly not a change of heart since his intention was still to give. This person, receives, שכר אמירה כשכר מעשה (a reward [for the] saying like a

---

1. The commentary *Minchat B'chorim* to *Tosefta Pe'ah* 4:17 states,

   אמר ליתן קודם שנתן אמר בפה נותנין לו שכר גם על אמירה מלבד המעשה

   ([if he said he would give before he gave, [meaning] he said out loud [lit. with his mouth] we also give him a reward for the saying, besides the deed). It should be noted that this may be an important distinction as,

   אמר שמואל גמר בלבו צריך שיוציא בשפתיו שנאמר לבטא בשפתים

   (Sh'muel said, if he decided in his mind, he must utter it with his lips, for it is said 'to utter with the lips (*Vayikra* 5:4)) (*Sh'vu'ot* 26b) for if not, then 'an oath in the mind is not an oath' (*ibid., Soncino Hebrew-English Ed.*, note c(3)). Rashi explains of the verse in *Vayikra* בשפים ולא בלב (with his lips and not [merely] in his heart). Verbalising the intention is thus of key importance.
2. BLOCH, *op. cit.*, p.54, Steinsaltz notes that בל תאחר, the prohibition against delaying a sacrifice that one has pledged was 'extended to cover pledges to charity and the like which must also be honoured within a [set] period of time'. (STEINSALTZ, *op. cit.*, p.171).
3. BLOCH, *op. cit.*, p.54.
4. NEUSNER, *op. cit.*, p.294.

reward [for the] deed). It may be from the use of the preposition כ (as, like) that the Rabbis saw each reward as equal in size, or it may just mean 'instead of'. Lieberman records an opinion that, ששכר דיבור הוא פחות משכר מעשה (that the reward [for the] speaking is <u>less</u> than the reward [for the] deed),[1] however little other comment is made in this direction.

The most difficult element of this case, however, is that it is in conflict with another strand of thought from the *Tannaim*. We have already noted, by reference to *Tosefta Pe'ah* 1:4, that God will transform even a good thought into reality,[2] so how can we possibly have a situation where, אמר ליתן ולא הספיק בידו (he said [he intended] to give and it was <u>not</u> sufficiently in his power [to do so]).

This may be explained by looking further at the meaning of לא הספיק בידו. Neusner renders 'he did not have enough'[3] which suggests that it is to do with lack of funds. However, since if he gave a single *p'rutah* his actual legal obligation would be discharged,[4] this seems a limited rendering.

Hammer suggests '[he] was then unable to do so'[5] which seems to be nearing the truth of the matter that this is something that lay outside of

---

1. LIEBERMAN, *op. cit.*, *Tosefta Ki-F'shuto* p.190, commenting on the passage as it occurs in *Tosefta Pe'ah* 4:17.
2. *Kiddushin* 40a similarly states, מחשבה טובה מצרפה למעשה (a good thought He joins it to a deed) and also, מחשבה שעושה פרי הקב"ה מצרפה למעשה (a thought that bears fruit the Holy One, blessed be He hardens to a deed), 'and both are rewarded' (*Soncino Hebrew-English Ed.*, note b(12)).
3. NEUSNER, *op. cit.*, p.294.
4. Though he may have pledged more than he was able to give. The *Amora* R, Isaac would later suggest that this was not possible since,
   כל הרודף אחר צדקה הקב"ה ממציא לו מעות ועושה בהן צדקה
   (all who seek to give *ts'dakah*, the Holy One Blessed be He provides for him the money, so that he might give *ts'dakah* with it (*Bava Batra* 9b)).
5. HAMMER, *op. cit.*, p.163.

his control. Jastrow understands the *hiphil* form in conjunction 'with בידו [as] to give sufficient time, or power, to allow an opportunity'.[1]

Since one is expected to follow up the pledge quickly, time may be a factor. It may also be that having made the announcement the opportunity may not present itself, though given the widespread poverty and the communal demand, this seems unlikely.[2]

Lack of time, funds or opportunity could all be valid reasons, but each are limiting in themselves. Given the use of ידי (his hand) in the phrase, it would seem that a translation that conveyed the wider sense that it was no longer in his power to accomplish, for whatever reason, seems more appropriate. Perhaps the *Tannaim* are implying that this now lies instead in the hands of God, who has thwarted, for some other reason, the good intention.[3]

---

1. JASTROW, *op. cit.*, p.1016.
2. The Amora R. Nachman b. Isaac would later argue that this too was impossible as, for one who intended to give,

    הקב"ה ממציא לו בני אדם המהוגנים לעשות להן צדקה כדי לקבל עליהם שכרו

    (the Holy One, Blessed be He would provide for him men who were fitting recipients of *ts'dakah* so that he receive his reward because of them).
3. There are similar ideas shown in a much later Rabbinic work, *Midrash T'hillim* 30, where King David is accorded the reward for the intention to build the Temple but because God had decided that he was too steeped in war, he was not allowed to build it. The good intention is thwarted, yet he still received a reward. The same passage also speaks of one who intended to give *ts'dakah*, that God will provide the means,

    מי עשה צדקה ולא נתתי לו קודם הדינרים מי שחשב בלבו לעשות מצוה
    ולא עשאה אני מעלה עליו כאלו עשאה שהרי דוד חשב לבנות בית המקדש
    ונקרא על שמו שנאמר מזמור שיר חנוכת הבית לדוד

    (who gave *ts'dakah* and I [God] had not given him first the *dinarim* to give with]? Whoever thought in his heart [i.e. intended] to do a *mitsvah* and did not do it, I accord it to him as if he had done it, for behold, David thought to build the Temple [and though I prevented him] it was called by his name, as it says 'A psalm, song of dedication to the House of [lit. to] David' (*T'hillim* 30:1)).

Lieberman notes a third view about rewards for intention,

אבל מאבות דר״ן מוכח שהיתה קיימת שיטה שאם אמר ליתן ולא הספיק בידו הרי מוכח שלא התנדב בגזרה מוחלטת משום שאחרת אי אפשר הקב״ה לא יפסיק בידו לפיכך הוא נענש אם לא נתן

(but from *Avot d'Rabbi Natan* it is clear that there existed a line [of thought] that if he said [he intended] to give and it was not in his power, it is clear that he did not [really] promise in a definite way, on account of [the fact] that after doing so it would be unthinkable that the Holy One Blessed be He should not enable him [to do so]. Therefore he is punished if he does not give).[1] Lieberman's reading of *Avot d'Rabbi Natan* suggests that if the intention was not followed by the deed, then in some way the promise to give was flawed at the outset and for this reason did not come to fruition and thus no reward would be given.

Our *Sifre* text then introduces a further expansion that even if he encouraged others to give then he gains a reward. A similar idea is detailed in a *baraita* preserved in *Bava Batra* 9a,

א״ר אלעזר גדול המעשה יותר מן העושה שנאמר והיה המעשה צדקה שלום ועבודת הצדקה השקט ובטח עד עולם

(R. El'azar said greater is the one who causes [the deed] than the doer, as it is said, 'and the one who causes *ts'dakah* [to be given] will have peace and the work of *ts'dakah* [i.e. the deed], [will be] quiet and surety forever'). Again we see a duality inherent, with two rewards, one for the 'causing' (of the intention to give) and one for the actual deed. This time, the reward for the 'causing' is greater than that of the deed itself.[2]

From an historical viewpoint, 'in each municipality, two collectors[3]

---

1. LIEBERMAN, *op. cit.*, p.190.
2. The blessing of 'peace' apparently outweighing 'quiet and surety', This perhaps reflects the early dictum of Hillel, in that,
   הוא היה אומר ... מרבה צדקה מרבה שלום (he (Hillel) was wont to say ... (he who gives) much charity, (his reward will be) much peace (*Avot* 2.8)).
3. והקופה נגבית בשנים (and the *kuppah* is collected by two (*Pe'ah* 8:7)), since

were appointed ... who made their rounds every Friday to the market and the shops and to private houses, taking the weekly collection for charity ... their duties were responsible and difficult [as] it is a harder thing to make others give than to give oneself and the desert and reward are correspondingly greater'.[1]

That the case of those who put the thought into other peoples minds to give is linked to our verse (*D'varim* 15:10) is perhaps a reflection of this particular social reality and is a reading back into Scripture rather than a derivation from it.

Indeed, Posner goes so far as to suggest that the job of these two *gabbay ts'dakah* (collectors of charity) was 'distasteful and humiliating'.[2] Maccoby adds that because of their position there was 'scope for slander against them'[3] from the community who may have distrusted them. Given these circumstances, they would therefore be even more deserving of reward.

The Biblical source for these ideas, appears to be Daniel 12:3, that ומצדיקי הרבים ככובים לעולם ועד (those who turn the many to righteousness [which the Rabbis have read as 'make the many give to *ts'dakah*' shall [shine] as the stars for ever and ever), and this has been

---

[ו]אין עושין שררה על הציבור בממון פחות משנים (we do not [allow authority] to be exercised over the congregation in [matters of] money [by] less than two [officers] (*Sh'kalim* 5:1)).

1. MOORE, *op. cit.*, p.174-175.
2. POSNER, *op. cit.*, p.174. This is possibly because of the idea that the 'courts could compel one who refuses to give charity ... even have the recalcitrant flogged, and should he still refuse [they] may appropriate the sum for charity', *ibid.*, p.168, also see *Gittin* 7a and *K'tubot* 49a), and thus the collectors could be viewed harshly by their neighbours as a sort of 'charity police'. That said, it was perhaps not as difficult as distributing the charity, for R. Jose said,

    יהי חלקי מגבאי צדקה ולא ממחלקי צדקה (may my portion be with those who collect charity and not with those who apportion charity (*Shabbat* 118b)), since 'it is very difficult to perform the latter with absolute impartiality, as personal predilections are apt to intervene' (*ibid.*, Soncino Hebrew-English Ed., note b(6)).

3. MACCOBY, *op. cit.*, p.66.

built upon in *Bava Batra* 8b to confirm the reward for this important social function.

A difficulty with this element of the *Sifre* text, however, lies with its potential conflict with a *mishnah* from *Pirkey Avot*, which discusses four types of person[1] who give to *ts'dakah*.

Sifre is quite explicit that,

לא אמר ליתן אבל אמר לאחרים תנו נותנים לו שכר על כך

([even if] he did not say he [intended] to give, but said to others, "Give!", we give him a reward for this). Yet *Avot* 5:13 states, אחרים והוא לא יתן עינו רעה בשלו ([he who desires] that others should give, but that he [himself] should not give, his <u>eye is evil</u>[2] towards that which is his own) and it is <u>only</u> of one of whom it is said, יתן ויתנו אחרים חסיד (he will give and he causes others to give, he is a pious person).

If the *mishnah* holds that one should both give and cause others to give to be worthy of the 'distinctive name of a Hasid',[3] and one who doesn't himself give is considered less than worthy, then *Sifre*, by promising a reward for only half of this equation, is clearly very concerned to demonstrate the reward for any charitable act.

Finally, the *Sifre* text extends the giving of reward to the extreme, by promising this 'merely' for engaging the poor with <u>good</u> words, *Sifre* gives נוח, whilst *Tosefta Pe'ah* 4:17 renders מניח, both suggesting good words are words that put the poor person's mind at rest or eases their burden in some way. Arguably, then, דברים טובים could be read literally as 'good words', words that are of value to the poor person as they are <u>useful</u> to him. Perhaps this is the giving of practical advice,

---

1. ארבע מדות בנותני צדקה ([there are] four types of character [lit. measures] in the giving of *ts'dakah*) (*Avot* 5:13).
2. i.e. he begrudges giving of his own.
3. *Avot* 5:13, *Soncino Hebrew-English Ed.*, note c(9).

rather than the 'kind'[1] or 'friendly'[2] words Neusner and Hammer suggest respectively, This is further supported by the parallel text in *Midrash Tannaim* which states, אבל מנחמו בדברים טובים (but comfort him with 'good' words).[3] They may be kind and friendly but perhaps, in order to offer real comfort they should contain some element of practical solution.

Whilst the other cases of receiving reward are readily accepted, there appears to have been a realisation amongst the *Tannaim* that a reward for speaking words only could be considered an odd lesson to draw. This is shown by their use of מניין (from where [do we learn]?) and the framing of this exegesis as a question, rather than a statement.[4]

דבר is, on this occasion, held to mean actual 'words' so that we can read, ... כי בגלל הדבר הזה (for because of this word). However unlike the earlier words with which we open the discussion presumably to give him a gift or a loan,[5] these words appear to be the sole offering to the poor man with no promise of any funds involved.

Whilst the exegetical link through דבר is clear, it is by reference to this concept in other sources that we can perhaps see why this opinion is held by the *Tannaim*.

Bloch notes that 'a cordial reception and kind words of sympathy may do more for an indigent than a monetary contribution'.[6] He draws here on *Avot d'Rabbi Natan*'s understanding of Shammai's dictum,

---

1. HAMMER, *op. cit.*, p.163.
2. NEUSNER, *op. cit.*, p.294.
3. *Midrash Tannaim* to *D'varim* 15: 10.
4. Hammer notes that the 'interrogative form is introduced by the word *minayin*, "from whence?". The question is asked, what is the Scriptural source of a known practice?' (HAMMER, *op. cit.*, p.11), or in this case Scriptural support for an opinion that is held.
5. See section 5.
6. BLOCH, *op. cit.*, p.54.

והוי מקבל את כל אדם בסבר פנים יפות (receive all men with a cheerful face).[1] This, it is argued, refers to receiving a petitioner for alms, since,

המקבל את חבירו בסבר פנים יפות אפי' לא נותן לו כלום מעלה עליו הכתוב כאילו נתן לא כל מתנות טובות בעולם

(one who receives his fellow with a cheerful face, even if he gives him nothing, Scripture accords it to him as if he gave him all the fine gifts that are in the world).[2]

Indeed there may be occasions where 'good words' help the poor person more than giving him money as the words themselves might spur him to self-sufficiency, the ultimate ideal of Jewish charity.

Further, a similar text in *Midrash Tannaim* which speaks of one who has nothing to give explains,

שאם אין ידך ליתן לו פתח לו בדברים ואומר לו בני תצא נפשי עליך שאין בידי ליתן לך וה"א ותפק לרעב נפשך

(that if there is not in your hand [funds] to give to him, open to him with words and say to him, my son, my soul will go out to you, for there is not in my hand to give to you, as it says 'and you will draw out to the hungry your soul' (*Y'shayah* 58:10)).[3]

This text shows that to 'draw out thy soul to the hungry' means giving the poor your time, concern and possibly advice, It also provides a reason why such actions are held to merit a reward, for this is prescribed by the prophet Y'shayah as the action to take when

---

1. *Avot* 1:15.
2. *Avot d'Rabbi Natan* 13:4.
3. *Midrash Tannaim* to *D'varim* 15:8. A similar citation is made by an Amoraic Sage in *Vayikra Rabbah* 34:15, אר"ל אם אין לך ליתן לו נחמו בדברים (Resh Lakish said, if you do not have [anything] to give to him comfort him with words). *Bava Batra* 91b goes further, stating that,

[ו]אמר רבי יצחק ... והמפייסו בדברים נתברך בי"א ברכות (R. Yitschak said ... but he that quietens him [i.e. puts him at ease] is blessed with eleven blessings).

encountering a poor person.[1]

Though we have now considered all the cases laid out by the *Sifre* text and though Neusner states that this contains 'all the possibilities of the case',[2] two cases are, in fact, missing. The first is one who willfully goes back on his word and does not give and the second is that of one who gave without intention.

The first of these is relatively easy to dismiss. Such a person would be breaking the commandment to give and would be, שהוא פושט ידו וחזור וקופצה (one that stretches his hand to give then closes it).[3] He would clearly receive no reward and would, in fact, be punished.

The second case is worth further exploration. Given that, for the *Tannaim* the intention to perform the commandment appears to be of almost equal importance to the deed itself, we could understand its omission from this section. However, it is not the case that this is ignored entirely, for elsewhere in *Sifre* we find that,

אמר רבי אלעזר בן עזריה מנין למאבד סלע מידו ומצאה עני והלך ונתפרנס בה מעלה עליו הכתוב כאילו זכה תלמוד לומר לגר ליתום ולאלמנה יהיה

(Rabbi *El'azar* ben Azaryah[4] said, from where [do we learn] that for one who loses a *sela* [coin] and a poor man finds it and goes and supports himself by it, Scripture accords it to him [i.e. the man who lost the coin] as if it was [a] meritorious [deed]'? From the verse 'It shall be for the stranger, for the fatherless and for the widow [that the Lord your

---

1. For the *Tannaim* 'Zedakah [was] not only measured by concrete, efficacious action. It also involved ... listening and sharing in the pain of the person in need irrespective of one's ability to solve or ameliorate the problematic conditions at hand' (HARTMAN & MARX, *op. cit.*, p.49).
2. NEUSNER, *op. cit.*, p.294.
3. *Sifre Piska* 116 to *D'varim* 15: 7. See section 2 for discussion.
4. 2nd generation *Tanna*, see STRACK & STEMBERGER, *op. cit.*, p.78.

God may bless you in all the work of your hands]').[1]

By drawing on a verse similar to *D'varim* 15:10, this *Piska* interprets בכל מעשה ידך (in all the deeds of your hands),[2] to allow even a clearly unintentional deed to merit reward.

Both from our *Sifre* passage and the other works quoted above, there is clearly an overwhelming concern amongst the *Tannaim* to both demonstrate and magnify the reward attendant on the *mitsvah* of *ts'dakah*.[3] Whilst each individual case may have its own explanation, such as the need to improve the status of the charity collectors to be sure of willing volunteers for the post,[4] the overall reason for this concern is not clear. This concern is particularly noticeable when it is considered that the early Rabbis were keen to point out that one should not carry out the *mitsvot* with a mind to reward, for example,

---

1. *Sifre Piska* 283 to *D'varim* 24:19. This follows Hammer's understanding of how the proof is reached from the rest of the verse not cited. The *Tannaim* may have been drawing on יהיה (it will be [to them], in that because the stranger, widows or orphans shall have the money regardless of how it came to them, the *mitsvah* has been accomplished and hence the reward is given. That said, the text does still go on to emphasise the Rabbis' 'preference' for a considered act,

   והלא דברים קל וחומר אם מי שלא נתכוון לזכות וזכה מעלה הכתוב עליו
   כאילו זכה המתכוון לזכות וזכה על אחת כמה וכמה

   (and is not this matter [an example of] *kal vachomer* [an inference from the minor to the major]. If one who does not intend to perform a meritorious deed, Scripture accounts it upon him as if he was meritorious, one who did intend to be meritorious, upon [such a] person, how much more so).
2. *D'varim* 24:19.
3. And even rewards generally, for though quoted in the much later work, *Midrash T'hillim*, and not specifically about *ts'dakah*, the Tannaitic Sage, Rabbi Shim'on bar Yochai goes even further and suggests that,

   ישב אדם ולא עבירה נותנין לו שכר כעושה מצוה ([if] a man sits and does not transgress, we give him a reward like one who does a commandment) (*Midrash T'hillim* 1) the implication being that merely the avoidance of sin merits a positive reward!
4. Maccoby notes that 'the collectors were voluntary communal workers', (MACCOBY, *op. cit.*, p.66).

אנטיגונוס איש סוכו ... היה אומר אל תהיו כעבדים המשמשין את הרב על מנת לקבל פרס אלא הוו כעבדים המשמשין את הרב שלא על מנת לקבל פרס

(Antigonus a man of Socho ... was wont to say, 'do not be like a slave who serves the master on the expectation of receiving a reward, rather be like a slave who does not serve on the expectation of receiving a reward').[1]

The Sages may instead have been drawing on a long established tradition that since 'Charity to the poor is equated with "lending to the Lord [and of such actions it is said] his good deeds will repay unto him"'.[2]

Further, 'the virtue of charity and the fact that it deserves reward from God is stressed over and over in the arguments in the book of Job'.[3] Such clear Biblical support would have allowed much discussion over the merits of even the smallest charitable act.

---

1. *Avot* 1:1. Cohen notes that 'whilst the doctrine or reward and punishment figures prominently in Talmudic teachings, nevertheless it is exhorted again and again that the service of God must be disinterested and His commandments observed from pure motives' (COHEN, *op. cit.*, p.120).
2. POSNER, *op. cit.*, p.166, from *Mishley* 19:17 which reads,
   מלוה ה' חונן דל וגמלו ישלם לו([he] lends to the Lord, [he who deals] graciously with the poor, and that which he gives, will be restored to him).
3. For example, *Iyyov* 29:11-14 gives,
   כי אזן שמעה ותאשרני ועין ראתה ותעידני: כי־אמלט עני משוע ויתום ולא־עזר לו: ברכת אבד עלי תבא ולב אלמנה ארנן: צדק לבשתי וילבשני כמעיל וצניף משפטי:
   (when the ear heard me it blessed me and [when] the eye saw me it gave witness to me for I delivered the poor that cried and the orphan who had none to help him. The blessing of he that [was ready to] perish came upon me and I caused the heart of the widow to sing. I dressed in righteousness and my justice clothed me as a robe and diadem). Iyyov is himself singled out as a champion of *ts'dakah* by the earliest Rabbis, even though he does not appear to have been rewarded as one might have expected.

Most likely the Rabbis are reflecting the harsh economic climate and realistically assessing that though many people would have the best of intentions to give they were just unable to do so, Such people would have a very real concern that they would be punished for not giving and the Rabbis are utilising the Biblical text to offer re-assurance that this would not be the case. Hammer notes the presence of an overriding theme within *Sifre* that tends to 'soften the punishment and accentuate the comfort and restoration'[1] so that 'whilst the sections on rebuke [in *D'varim* and *Sifre* are replete with condemnation of Israel, *Sifre* misses no opportunity to praise the people and to stress God's positive relationship to them'.[2] At a time when the social and political situation looked bleak, the stress on reward may have been 'to reassure the Jewish people in their hour of tragedy and depression'[3] that they were still worthy of merit and future reward if they followed God's will, both generally, and specifically regarding the giving of *ts'dakah*. We should take this lesson to heart today and recognise the positive aspects of the *mitsvah* for the reward does not have to be physical. More likely it will be psychological - we just feel better when we give.

---

1. HAMMER, *op, cit.*, p.16.
2. *Ibid.*
3. *Ibid.*, p.17.

Section 13 - 'the needy will never cease'

כי לא יחדל **אביון** מקרב הארץ ולהלן הוא אומר אפס כי לא יהיה בך אביון כיצד נתקיימו שני כתובים הללו בזמן שאתם עושים רצונו של מקום אביונים באחרים וכשאין אתם עושים רצונו של מקום אביונים בכם

('For the needy will never cease from the midst of the Earth'. But elsewhere it says 'howbeit there will not be amongst you a needy person'. How can both these two verses be fulfilled? At the time that you do the will of the Omnipresent [lit. The Place], the needy are amongst others and when you do not do the will of the Omnipresent, the needy are amongst you.)

For the Sages, a literal reading of *D'varim* 15:11 generates a conflict with the earlier verse, 15:4, requiring reconciliation. Logically, they ask, if the poor will never cease, how can a circumstance arise where there will not be amongst you a needy person? This would imply that *D'varim* 15:4 was at best redundant, at worst misleading!

The classic answer supplied by the commentators[1] is that this ideal is

---

1. For example Ramban to *D'varim* 15:11, explains,
   כי יהיה בך אביון אם שמוע תשמע בקול ה' אלקיך לשמור לעשות את כל המצוה
   ('for there will not be amongst you a needy [person]', [only] if you surely obey the voice of the Lord your God, to keep [and] to do this commandment'). Similarly Ibn Ezra to verse 4 states,
   אם היו כל ישראל או רובם שומעים בקול השם אז לא יהיה בך אביון (if all Israel or [even] most of them obeyed the voice of God, then 'there will not be amongst you a needy [person]').

achievable only if the conditions laid out in *D'varim* 15:5 are met;

רק אם שמוע תשמע בקול יהוה אלהיך לשמר לעשות את כל המצוה הזאת אשר אנכי מצוך היום

(only if you will surely obey [lit. listen to] the voice of your God to keep [and] to do all these commandments, which I command you this day).

Though the *Tannaim* in *Sifre* do not make specific reference to verse 5, their reasoning is very similar and the framing of their explanation, appears almost as a paraphrase of this verse. This may indeed have been the original rationale behind the explanation and could be an unspecified example of the hermeneutical rule of *davar halamed me'inyano* (a thing learnt from its context).[1]

There appears to be no parallel to these ideas in *Midrash* or *Talmud*, though in the *Targum Y'rushalmi*[2] to *D'varim* 15:11, the following is given,

אין נטרין הינון ישראל מצוות דאורייתא לא יהוי בהון מסכנין ברם אין שבקין הינון מצוותא דאורייתא ארום לא פסקין מסכנין בגו ארעא ...

(If Israel keep the commandments of the Torah, there will not be amongst them needy [people], but, if they forsake the commandments of the *Torah*, behold, the needy will not cease in the land ...).

The message is clear, עושים רצונו של מקום (doing the will of the

---

1. An argument derived from context, in that 'every Scripture passage which is close to another must be interpreted with respect to it' (STRACK & STEMBERGER, *op. cit.*, p.23).
2. Considered to have originated in Palestine, 'reckoned as belonging to rabbinic literature, because where they offer interpretation ... they do so within the rabbinic tradition'. Moreover 'the main influence on them ... [were] the rabbis of the second century CE', (MACCOBY, *op, cit.*, pp.29-30), the period with which we are largely concerned. Though ostensibly a translation into Aramaic the various *Targumim* also serve to clarify the meanings of passages and also contain a fair amount of Midrashicinterpretation.

Omnipresent) in *Sifre* is understood in this *Targum* as
נטריך ... מצוות דאורייתא (keeping ... the commandments of the
Torah), There is no doubt then what God's will entails, though one
could argue whether this implies adhering to the commandments
generally or specifically just those concerning *ts'dakah*.

Since Israel does not appear to be able to do either consistently,[1] it is
fairly pragmatic to expect that the poor will never cease. *D'varim* 15:4
is thus generally held to refer to some remote utopian ideal.[2]

It is also worth noting that this is the first occasion in our *midrash* that
God is mentioned other than in quotations from the Torah verses.[3] The
epithet the Sages choose to employ, המקום (lit. The Place), is often
rendered 'The Omnipresent' and is common in the Tannaitic sources.
However though this name of God could suggest a rather remote,
'everywhere' God, Urbach argues that 'the designation Maqom as it is
used in Rabbinic sources has no abstract, transcendental character, but,
on the contrary, expresses the nearness of man to God'.[4] If so, the use
of this name would be particularly apt in this exegesis since the Sages

---

1. 'It is here [verse 11] taken for granted that not for all time will all the people lead such an ideal life' (Ed. COHEN, A, *The Soncino Chumash*, The Soncino Press, London, 1983, p.1070, note 11). Plaut sees this as 'a realistic appraisal of Israel's limited capacity to live in all respects as holy people' (PLAUT, *op. cit.*, p. 1441).
2. Indeed this utopia may not even result in the removal of poverty, as one early *Amora* reports *D'varim* 15:11 on three occasions as evidence to suggest that even in the Messianic era poverty will not cease,

    דאמר שמואל אן בין העולם לימות המשיח אלא שיעבוד מלכויות בלבד שנ'
    כי לא יחדל אביון מקרב הארץ

    (*Sh'muel* said there is no difference between this world and the days of the Messiah other than the [removal of the] servitude to the kingdoms, alone, as it says 'for the poor will never cease from the Earth' (*Shabbat* 151b)). *Shabbat* 63a and *B'rachot* 34b give ... אלא שיעבוד גלויות ... (... other than the [removal of the] servitude of the exiles). It is worth noting that *Sh'muel* seems to be a loner in this opinion and for most Sages the Messianic era would have been thought to imply an end to poverty.
3. *D'varim* 15:7, 15:9 and 15:10.
4. URBACH, *op. cit.*, p 74.

are urging a nearness to God, through following his will.[1]

In our *midrash*, the *Tannaim* are also focusing on the fact that *D'varim* 4:11 refers to בך (amongst you) - which they stress implies amongst the children of Israel specifically,[2] whereas *D'varim* 15:11 is speaking of מקרב הארץ (from the midst of the Earth). Previously מארצך (from your land (*D'varim* 15:7)) was understood by the Rabbis to refer specifically to the Land, i.e. Israel.[3] Here, however, הארץ, a word that has many meanings, is deliberately taken in the wider sense of the Earth or the World. This is, in turn, held to imply all other nations, which allows the exegesis.

Having established that one verse implies Israel and one implies the rest of the nations, the *Tannaim* are able to argue, that keeping God's Law would mean that *D'varim* 15:4 applies and that there will be no poor amongst Israel, and with reference to 15:11, by extension, that the poor will be amongst the others.

Conversely, not keeping the commandments means that *D'varim* 15:4 does not apply and there will be poor amongst you, but not amongst others. This last element is not really implied by either verse and it would seem that nowhere do the nations enjoy even the possibility of escaping poverty.[4] Its presence as a possibility in our *midrash* may just be to give a literary balance to the statement rather than indicate an actual belief held by the *Tannaim*.

The *Tannaim* would be keen to emphasise the keeping of the

---

1. Often described as 'walking in God's ways'.
2. We have already seen בך being used to imply ולא באחרים (and not amongst others). See section 1.
3. See section 1 on the hierarchy of giving.
4. Hammer reports a prominent theme in *Sifre*, that whilst 'Israel is beloved [by God] and will be redeemed, the nations who have dealt cruelly with her are condemned and will suffer the consequences of their cruelty' (HAMMER, *op. cit.*, p.18). Perhaps they will suffer poverty come what may.

commandments to the people and this interpretation would lend support to their arguments. Moreover, employing this rationale could also help them explain the great poverty the people were experiencing by suggesting this was because Israel, collectively, was not keeping the commandments properly. This is a common enough theme in Rabbinic literature, utilised when the Sages were searching for an explanation as to why Israel was suffering whilst its enemies were apparently prospering.[1]

A similar, though later use of the potentially conflicting verses can be found in *Vayikra Rabbah*, though it provides a slightly different slant. Here, they are used to demonstrate how,
אף הכתובים חלקו כבוד לישראל (even Scripture. [lit. the Writings] apportioned honour to Israel), for,
ר' שמואל בר נחמן אמר תרתין שטין אפס כי לא יהיה בך אביון כשהוא בא לדבר בדבר של גנאי כי לא יחדל אביון מקרבכם אין כתיב כאן אלא מקרב הארץ
(R. Sh'muel bar Nachman,[2] said [there are] two principles [lit. two lines]: 'howbeit there will not be a needy [person] amongst you' (i.e. the positive statement applies to you - Israel) [but] when it comes to speak of a matter of disgrace, [such as] 'for the needy will never cease', it is not written here, 'out of your [i.e, Israel's] midst', rather lit says] 'from the midst of the Earth').[3]

This later text does crystalise our understanding of the two verses and may reflect the way the *Tannaim* also understood them when suggesting their exegesis.

For, the *Tannaim* there is a clear indication that *D'varim* 15:11 applies particularly to the other nations, though Israel can be, and realistically

---

1. For example, the destruction of the Temple is similarly often seen as being the direct result of the collective sins of Israel.
2. 3rd generation Palestinian *Amora*, (See STRACK & STEMBERGER, *op. cit.*, p.97).
3. *Vayikra Rabbah* 2:5.

usually are, also put in that category if they are not following God's commandments. The presence of *D'varim* 15:4, however, allows them to avoid that fate and offers a hope (however remote) of an end to poverty, that a straightforward reading of *D'varim* 15:11 might not otherwise imply.

Section 14 - 'good counsel I give to you'

על כן [מפני כן] אנכי מצוך לאמר עצה טובה אני נותן לך מטובתך

(**'Therefore I command you saying'**, 'therefore', because of this, '**I command you saying'**, good counsel I give to you for your [own] good).

The first comment by the *Tannaim* מפני כן (because of this) is absent from a number of manuscripts. It appears to be a simple clarification of meaning of על כן (therefore) to link this clause more firmly to the previous element of the verse, כי לא יחדל אביון מקרב הארץ (for the needy will not cease from the midst of the Earth).[1] The emphasis is that it is on account of this that the commandment is given as a permanent institution.

If it is so clearly a commandment, however, why then are the *Tannaim* suggesting that the Scriptural verse is also conveying good advice? Surely the force of the command is sufficient?

Hammer suggests that 'the extra word *saying* [לאמר] is interpreted as meaning 'to give advice'[2] giving us yet another example of the explanation of a potentially superfluous word in Scripture. Certainly the *Tannaim* argue elsewhere in *Sifre* that שאין ת״ל לאמר (that Scripture does not say 'saying' [except for a special purpose])[3] and

---

1. *D'varim* 15:11.
2. HAMMER, *op. cit.*, p.439, *Piska* 118, note 2.
3. *Sifre Piska* 26 to *D'varim* 3:23

there are many examples given where this word has been held to extend the meaning of the verse.[1]

Emek Han'tsiv, however, suggests the reason for this additional statement by the *Tannaim* is that,

זו שלא יחדל לכן היא מצוה ואם היה נחדל לעתים לא היה מצוה ליתן בעת שיהיו עניים אלא עצה טובה היא

(this is [because the needy] will never cease, therefore it is a commandment, but if it did cease at times [then] there would not be a commandment to give, so at [another] time that there were poor. then it would be [only] good advice).[2] Though *Emek Han'tsiv* suggests a reason for the statement with the link to *D'varim* 15:4,[3] 'the explanation for the presence of 'good counsel' does not seem satisfactory as it ignores the key word מטובתך (for your [own] good).[4]

Instead, one could argue that what the *Tannaim* are stressing is that whilst the commandment is for the good of the poor recipient and thus obligatory, even if there were no commandment at all, it would nonetheless be an advisable course of action to undertake as it would also be of benefit to the giver.

This benefit may be on a communal[5] level, such as the general reduction in poverty. More likely though, this refers to benefit on an <u>individual</u> basis. It could be a reference back to the lengthy

---

1. *Ibid.* However it should be noted that this is not always the case, for example see *Piska'ot* 5 and 16, where no additional meaning is ascribed to the presence of לאמר (saying) in the verse.
2. *Emek Han'tsiv* to *Piska* 118.
3. See section 13 for discussion of this link.
4. Many texts amend this to לטובתך.
5. We cannot assume that the singular form מטובתך (for your [own] good) is to be read as implying an individual, as it may be referring to the people of Israel as a communal entity as was the case with בך (amongst you) in *D'varim* 15:7, in its context.

deliberations on the rewards of giving[1] which certainly would make giving *ts'dakah* something for your own benefit. Taking a more negative view, it could also be related to the discussion of failure to give constituting a sin,[2] the avoidance of which would also be to the giver's benefit. In either instance, the gaining of reward or avoidance of punishment, this would be seen to represent sound advice, over and above the commandment to give.

---

1. See section 12.
2. See section 9.

Section 15 - 'if it is fitting'

פתוח תפתח את ידך לאחיך לעניך לאביונך למה נאמרו כולם הראוי ליתן לו פת נותנים לו פת עיסה נותנים לו עיסה מעה נותנים לו מעה להאכילו בתוך פיו מאכילים אותו בתוך פיו

('You will surely open your hand to your brother, to your poor land] to your needy'. Why does it say all of these [categories]? [It teaches[1] that if] it is fitting to give him a piece of bread we give him a piece of bread, a quantity of flour, we give him a quantity of flour, a *m'ah* [coin] we give him a *m'ah* [coin], [or if the need is] to place food into his mouth, we place food into his mouth).

We have already seen[2] that this section of text is paralleled in *Tosefta Pe'ah* 4:10, where it adds, היה משתמש בכלי מילת נותנים לו כלי מילת (if he were used to woollen garments, we give him woollen garments), but otherwise the examples shown above are repeated, albeit in a different order.

In *Tosefta Pe'ah* this text served as a precurser to, די מחסרו אשר יחסר לו (appropriate to his lack which is lacking to him)[3] and in this context was clearly concerned to reflect the more 'usual' needs of the poor person as opposed to the 'unusual' (though nonetheless still appropriate) requirements of the עני בן טובים (poor person of good family).

---

1. The GR"A in his emendations suggests that this should read מגיד הכתוב (Scripture teaches).
2. See section 5.
3. *D'varim* 15:8. See section 5.

In *Sifre* however, this tradition has been separated from *D'varim* 15:8 and is instead appended to 15:11, where the *Tannaim* utilise it to explain the apparently superfluous use of synonyms.[1]

We have already seen that the various names for the poor carried different meanings for the *Tannaim*[2] and here the suggestion is that different types of poor will have different needs which should be met. The examples shown, and, including the one from the *Tosefta* version, speak of the provision of food, clothing and money, the basic and more usual charity requirements of the poor. Some poor may require one or all of these and that which is given should be appropriate to circumstance. The last example is perhaps a reference to a disabled or very elderly person who has a particular need in relation to the food given to him

Though the order does vary between the two texts, there is a sense, in the *Sifre* text at least, of increasing degrees of provision, coupled with a movement from communal to more personal responsibility. The gift of food develops from a small portion of bread, to flour for a full meal. The gift of money could be a loan (or at least the pretense of one) and represent a higher level of involvement with the poor person than their taking of food from the communal plate. The final example of caring physically for a disabled or elderly person by literally 'spoon-feeding' them, would perhaps require a greater personal involvement and level of *ts'dakah* giving of them all. Where the provision of clothing would fit in to this scale, is a matter for debate, as is the reason for its absence from the *Sifre* text.

This section thus provides further evidence that the *Tannaim* were keen to promote the universal application of the principle that *ts'dakah* was

---

1. Hammer explains that 'there are two formulaic verses which deal with the question of seemingly superfluous verses ... one [beginning] *lammah ne'emar* ...' (HAMMER, *op. cit.*, p.13).
2. See section 1 for discussion of the various names given to the poor.

appropriate to the specific individual, as well as being of sufficient quantity.

Despite this emphasis in *Sifre*, however, there may have been some dissent from this view. *Y'rushalmi Pe'ah* 8:7 states,

תני משתמש בכלי זהב נותנין לו כלי כסף כלי כסף נותנין לו כלי נחושת כלי נחושת נותנין לו כלי זכוכית

(it was taught [in a Tannaitic *baraita*, that if] he used vessels of gold, we give him vessels of silver, vessels of silver we give him vessels of brass, vessels of brass, we give him vessels of glass).

Instead of matching needs, this *baraita* seems to suggest that the poor person reduce their expectation, and that the community wean them off their former requirements. However, the *baraita* that the *Y'rushalmi* is citing is, according to the commentary *Toldot Yitschak*, to be found in a variant in *Tosefta Pe'ah* 4:11, which gives,

היה משתמש בכלי זהב מוכרין ומשתמש בכלי כסף בכלי כסף מוכרין ומשתמש בכלי נחושת בכלי נחושת מוכרין ומשתמש בכלי זכוכית

(if he was used to using vessels of gold, he sells them and uses vessels of silver, vessels of silver, he sells them and uses vessels of brass, vessels of brass, he sells them and uses vessels of glass).

The *Tosefta* text is quite clearly concerned with the poor person selling his possessions and not with the gifts of such vessels to the poor. This is further clarified by what precedes this *baraita* as it appears in *K'tubot* 68a,

תני חתם אין מחייבין אותו למכור ביתו ואת כלי תשמישו (it is taught there,[1] [that] we do not bind him [i.e. the poor person) to sell his house [or] his vessels of service [i.e. household utensils]). The discussion is clearly over whether a poor person is expected to sell his goods, the proceeds of which might take him above the minimum of

---

1. In *Mishnah Pe'ah* 8:8.

200 *zuzim* by which he would no longer be classified as poor according to the Rabbinic definition of the term.[1]

It is quite possible then that the version of the *baraita* found in the *Y'rushalmi* is a poorer transmission and not a negation of the *Sifre* view of providing appropriate *ts'dakah*.

Of potentially greater conflict however, is a tradition quoted in *Avot d'Rabbi Natan* 21a(1),

אתה יושב ושוהה בביתך ואורחין נכנים אצלך את שדרכו לאכול פת חטין האכילתו פת חטין את שדרכו לאכול בשר האכילתו בשר את שדרכו לשתות יין השקיתו יין

(you i.e. Iyyov] sit and wait in your house and guests[2] come in to you. For one who was accustomed to eat wheaten bread, you fed him wheaten bread, for one who was accustomed to eat meat, you fed him meat, [and] for one who was accustomed to drink wine, you gave him wine [to drink]).

Iyyov is clearly acting in a manner that the *Tannaim* of *Sifre* would applaud, yet this generosity was apparently insufficient to avert the calamities that befell him. When he questions why this should be the case, we learn that,

אעפ״כ א״ל הקב״ה לאיוב עדיין לא הגעת [לחצי שיעור] של אברהם ... אברהם לא עשה כן אלא יושב ומהדר בעולם וכשימצא

---

1. מי שיש לו מאתים זוז לא יטול לקט שכחה ופאה ומעשר שני (He that has 200 *zuzim* does not take from the gleanings, the forgotten sheaf, the *pe'ah* (corner [of the field] or the poor man's tithe (*ibid.*)), The *Amoraim* deal with the conflict between the opposing *baraitot*, by suggesting that you may make him sell (i.e, the *Tosefta* version) only applies to one who has made a false claim, whereas the statement that one does not make him sell (i.e. the *Mishnah* version) applies to one whose claim is valid. See *K'tubot* 68a.
2. Often employed as a euphemism for the poor. This may stem from the instruction to [ו]היו עניים בני ביתך (let the poor be members [lit. sons] of your household (*Avot* 1:5)).

אורחין מכניסן בתוך ביתו את שאין דרכו לאכול פת חטין האכילתו
פת חטין את שאין דרכו לאכול בשר האכילתו בשר ואת שאין דרכו
לשתות יין השקהו יין

(even if you did all this [i.e. feed and clothe the poor], the Holy One blessed be he said to Iyyov, nonetheless you have not attained a half of the hospitality of Avraham ... [because] Avraham did not do so, rather he would wander about and when he found 'guests', he would bring them into his house [and] to one who was unaccustomed to eat wheaten bread, he fed him wheaten bread, for one who was unaccustomed to eat meat, he fed him meat [and] for one who was unaccustomed to drink wine, he gave him wine [to drink]),

Avraham's behaviour is held up here as the ideal and as such is in conflict with *Sifre* in that it suggests one should do <u>more</u> than merely restore what is missing in one's giving of *ts'dakah*, However *Avot d'Rabbi Natan* 'contains material which is unique in Talmudic literature'[1] and perhaps it was merely an illustrative ethical maxim which, whilst promoting a further dimension to giving, was primarily concerned with demonstrating Avraham's 'specialness'[2] and not expected to represent the expected behaviour of appropriate giving, as recommended in *Sifre*. But that doesn't mean we might not want to strive to emulate the example of Avraham.

---

1. CASHDAN, E, *Introduction to Avot d'Rabbi Natan, Soncino Hebrew-English Ed.*, Soncino Press, London 1984.
2. Avraham is held by the Rabbis to be Scripture's chief proponent of the giving of hospitality, based on his actions in *B'reshit* 18, when visited by three 'angels', for example, והנה שלשה אנשים נצוים עליו וירא וירץ לקראתם (and behold three men were standing before him, and he [Avraham] saw them <u>and he ran</u> to greet them (*B'reshit* 18:2)), suggesting his eagerness to do a good deed.

Overview

Moore notes of our *Sifre* passage that 'most of [the] fine doctrine about charity is interpreted into the text, not out of it ... the fundamentals of Jewish teaching on the subject - are here ingeniously worked into a single passage only a few verses long.'[1]

He is, in this statement, partly correct, in that we have seen some instances above where the lesson has been 'forced' (for want of a better word) out of Scripture to match the common practice of the time.[2] In other cases, however, Scripture has been used as a springboard for development of the *Halachah*, with the derivation being an expansion on the Biblical subject matter and a way for the Sages to shape practice. In yet other cases, a lesson has been suggested largely to account for a seeming redundancy in the text.

In this relatively short passage, based on a section of Scripture primarily concerned with the one specific example of <u>lending</u> (rather then giving) before the Sabbatical year, the *Tannaim* have nonetheless raised a multitude of issues related to the giving of *ts'dakah*.

Throughout, one is struck by the overwhelming <u>fairness</u> and <u>balance</u> that forms the basis of their exegesis. This is combined with an underlying sense of <u>realism</u> as to what the community, and the individuals who constitute it, could be expected to do to counter the problem of poverty.

The concern of the *Tannaim* to demonstrate priority in the giving of *ts'dakah* from *D'varim* 15:7 gives us at once their ideal, where the

---

1. MOORE, *op. cit.*, p.168.
2. '[interpreting] the Mosaic legislation on the subject of charity in its spirit, sometimes, to our notions of exegesis, straining the letter in doing so' (*ibid.*, p.165).

neediest is put at the forefront, regardless of who it is. This is tempered, however, by the Sages' own understanding of reality. People would be concerned about their own family, their own neighbours and their own country before others and the *Halachah* therefore reflects this. Any other suggestion would be against human nature and difficult, if not impossible, to implement.

The harsh treatment of the needy person begging at the door, coupled with the Sages attempts to widen the application of the whole passage beyond that of loaning to the poor, reflects their concern to make Scripture fit into their own established formalised communal structure of giving *ts'dakah*, one which had developed considerably since the agricultural gifts to which the Torah specifically refers.[1]

However, despite the fact that the giver is largely viewed collectively as the community, giving through the *kuppah* and *tamchui*, the Sages are very keen to utilise the Biblical verses to maintain the individualism of the poor recipient. Two large sections of our *Sifre* text[2] suggest that the Biblical text is prompting us to consider the individual requirements of the needy person and as far as possible match those needs through appropriate giving. To really think about the recipient as a person. Perhaps the *Tannaim* sensed a danger that the communal forms of *ts'dakah* were, to and extent, 'de-personalising' the act, where funds were contributed for the wider good with little consideration being given to the individual recipient and what it was that he or she really lacked.[3]

---

1. The forgotten sheaf, the corner of the field etc. - all forms that readily identified the poor person, causing possible shame and which, as we have noted, were less applicable when Jews became a more urban population.
2. Though, as noted these sections may originally have been linked, see *Tosefta Pe'ah* 4:10.
3. For example in *Y'rushalmi Pe'ah* 8:8, the *Amora*, R. Yonah says,
אשרי נותן לדל אין כתיב כאן אלא אשרי משכיל אל דל ('Happy [is the one] who gives to the poor', it is not written here [in *T'hillim* 41:21] rather [it is written] 'Happy is the one who [gives] consideration to the poor'), i.e. who thinks about their plight and needs.

To a certain extent, aside from material wealth, what a poor person can also lack is self-respect, since poverty could easily lead to a loss of dignity. The Rabbis recognised this problem too, and attempted to solve it with their exhortations that aside from giving appropriately and on a frequent basis, the way in which one gave was equally important.[1] The reference to the לשכת חשאים (Chamber of Secrets) and their discussions over how the approach to the poor person should be made (either as a loan or a gift) betray their anxiousness to <u>avoid shaming</u> the recipient in any way.

Both these stimuli towards appropriate giving and avoiding shaming the poor are brought into sharp focus through our *Sifre* passage by direct or indirect reference to the special case of the עני בן טובים (poor person of good family). As noted through this study, this may indicate that there was a growing number of such poor due to the prevailing economic and political conditions. Though their case is more extreme than the norm, the idea of providing appropriate *ts'dakah* in a suitable manner still prevails.

Ts'dakah is thus viewed by the *Tannaim* as essentially 'restoring a God willed balance to the human realm'[2] reflecting the root of the word צדק (justice) implying that these gifts (like the Biblical *pe'ah*, *leket* etc.) were rightfully the property of the poor,[3] and thus giving is obligatory.

This concept of balance is also witnessed in the punishment prescribed for not giving. In the Biblical text failure to give is clearly stated to be a sin and though the *Tannaim* could be accused of exaggerating somewhat by linking it with idolatry, the punishment nonetheless

---

1. What is pertinent is that [the] non-economic variable of deprivation [i.e. *bushah* (shame)] is taken seriously in determining *zedakah* priorities' (HARTMAN & MARX, *op. cit.*, p.50).
2. PLAUT, *op. cit.*, p.1461.
3. רבי אלעזר איש ברתותא אומר תן לו משלו שאתה ושלך שלו (R. El'azar a man of Bertota said, give unto Him what is His seeing that what you have are His (*Avot* 3: 7)).

follows the well established principle of *middah k'neged middah* (measure for measure). The account is, however, rendered by God, not an earthly court and God quite clearly sides with the poor person in this transaction since there is no real excuse for not giving, as even a small amount is acceptable and would avoid you being labelled as one who is בליעל or who has an 'evil eye'.

Where the *Tannaim* do depart from a balanced view, is in their treatment of the rewards for giving *ts'dakah*. There can be no doubt that the pressure on a person to withhold funds from the communal collection or from individuals that petitioned them was great, as they would have had their own financial difficulties. Other Tannaitic sources, as noted, suggest that *mitsvot* should be carried out לשם שמים (for the sake of heaven)[1] with no thought to reward, yet the emphasis on reward for giving is heavy in *Sifre*, both for the actual giving and encouraging others.

Again, the *Tannaim* may have realistically assessed that the 'stick' of future punishment was insufficient[2] and that the 'carrot' of greater reward was required. The phrasing of the Biblical text allowed them to expand on the reward and promise much for varying degrees of the *ts'dakah* act. This was perhaps both to bolster the spirits of the potential giver and to reinforce in the minds of those who gave that they had done the right thing; for though they have parted with their money by giving, it was nonetheless also מטובתך (for [their own] benefit[3] - either materialistically or phsychologically.

Mentioned during the debate over rewards and intimated elsewhere in the passage is the Tannaitic stress that all acts are held to have two

---

1. וכל מעשיך יהיה לשם שמים (and all your deeds should be for the sake of heaven (*Avot* 2:12)). *Sifre* to *D'varim* 6:5 also notes that the idea is that one should עשה מאהבה (act out of love [of God]).
2. As we have already noted the wicked appeared to be prospering at that time.
3. *Sifre* to D'varim 15:11.

components, the intention (*kavannah*) and the deed (*ma'aseh*) itself - *ts'dakah* is no exception. We have already seen that one is expected to consider the poor, their needs and their status and perhaps the importance the *Tannaim* ascribe to the intention to give is, in part, to ensure the act is carefully considered and carried out in the correct manner and spirit, with a cheerful face and 'good words'. Moreover these 'good words' could be of greater benefit than the gift of money, clothing or food if they contributed sound advice that led to self-sufficiency.

A final injection of realism by the *Tannaim* is shown in their interpretation of two of the occurrences of the infinitive absolute. One is expected to 'open' or 'give', אפילו מאה פעמים (even one hundred times). This requirement for frequent giving bears witness to the great poverty that was facing the Jews during that period under Roman domination and also Sages understanding that the problem was not going to go away; that, לא יחדל האביון מקרב הארץ (the needy will never cease from the midst of the Land).[1] It also teaches that *ts'dakah* is a continuous *mitsvah* that is never ever completed, thus negating the modern idiom - 'I gave already' as a poor excuse.

Finally, though the *Tannaim* through our *Sifre* text, present largely formal, realistic and balanced views they do, however, offer one small hope of a time where poverty could end. As one would expect, from a text primarily concerned with determining the *halachah*, this utopia is only achievable, בזמן שאתם עושים רצונו של מקום (in a time when you [collectively] do the will [i.e. the commandments] of the Omnipresent).

---

1. *D'varim* 15:11. 2, *Sifre* to *D'varim* 15:11.

It seems that whilst one individual can and should always try to make a difference, both giving themselves and encouraging others to give, only properly organised and sustained collective effort on the part of the whole community on a major scale can really ever hope to eradicate poverty.

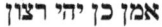

Appendix 1
Maimonides 'ladder' of *ts'dakah* giving

The 'Eight Degrees of Charity' from *Hilchot Matt'not Aniyyim* 10:1,7-14 (Maimonides, *Mishneh Torah*, Laws of Gifts to the Poor).

ז שמנה מעלות יש בצדקה זו למעלה מזו מעלה גדולה שאין למעלה
ממנה זה המחזיק ביד ישראל שמך ונותן לו מתנה או הלואה או
עושה עמו שותפות או ממציא לו מלאכה כדי לחזק את ידו עד שלא
יצטרך לבריות לשאול ועל זה נאמר והחזקת בו גר ותושב וחי עמך
כלומר החזק בו עד שלא יפול ויצטרך. ח פחות מזה הנותן צדקה
לעניים ולא ידע למי נתן ולא ידע העני ממי לקח שהרי זו מצוה
לשמה כגון לשכת חשאים שהיתה במקדש שהיו הצדיקים נותנין
בה בחשאי והעניים בני טובים מתפרנסין ממנה בחשאי וקרוב לזה
הנותן לתוך קופה של צדקה ולא יתן אדם לתוך קופה של צדקה אלא
אם כן יודע שהממונה נאמן וחכם ויודע להנהיג כשורה כר׳ חנניה
בן תרדיון. ט פחות מזה שידע הנותן למי יתן ולא ידע העני ממי
לקח כגון גדולי החחכמים שהיו הולכין בסתר ומשליכין המעות
בפתחי העניים וכזה ראוי לעשות ומעלה טובה היא אם אין הממונין
בצדקה נוהגין כשורה. י פחות מזה שידע העני ממי נטל ולא ידע
הנותן כגון גדולי החכמים שהיו צוררים המעות בסדיניהן ומפשילין
לאחוריהן ובאין העניים ונוטלין כדי שלא יהיה להן בושה. יא פחות
מזה שיתן לו בידו קודם שישאל. יב פחות מזה שיתן לו אחר
שישאל. יג פחות מזה שיתן לו פחות מן הראוי בסבר פנים יפות.
יד פחות מזה שיתן לו בעצב.

7: There are eight levels in *ts'dakah,* each higher than the other. The greatest level, where there is no higher level is to strengthen the hand of the Jew who is lowly, and give him a gift or a loan or make with him a partnership or find him some work, so as to strengthen his hand, such that he need ask anything of anyone. And of this it is said 'You shall strengthen the stranger and the dweller in your midst and live with him'[1] (*Vayikra* 25:35) in other words strengthen him so he does not fall and be needy. **8:** Less than this is the giver of *ts'dakah* to the poor and he does not know to whom he gives, nor does the poor person know

---

1. *Vayikra* 25:35.

from whom he takes - this is a *mitsvah* for the same of heaven, similar to the Chamber of Secrets that was in the Temple, where the righteous gave therein in secret and the poor of good family were provided a living from it in secret. And next to this is giving into the communal *ts'dakah* fund. One should not put into the box unless he knows that the one responsible for the box is faithful and wise and a proper leader like Rabbi Chananya ben Teradyon.[1] **9:** Less than this is that the giver knows to whom he gives but the poor person does not know from whom he takes, similar to the great wise ones who went in secret and put coins through the doors of the poor and this is something fitting to do and this is a good level if the administrators of the *ts'dakah* [funds] are accustomed [to act] properly. **10:** Less than this is that the poor person knows from whom takes gives but the giver does not know [to whom he gives] similar to the great wise ones who tied up the money in the sheets raised up behind them and the poor came and took so that they weren't ashamed. **11:** Less than this, is that he gave into his hand before he was asked. **12:** Less than this, is that he gave him after he was asked. **13:** Less than this is that he gave him less than was fitting but with a cheerful countenance. **14:** Less than this is that he gave him with grudgingly.[2]

---

1. Rabbi Chananya ben Teradyon, a 3rd Generation *Tanna* who was known as a man with an overriding concern for the poor. His efforts to raise funds on their behalf were legendary. He became a victim of the Romans. Before they burned him at the stake, the Romans wrapped his body in a Torah scroll and packed tufts of water-soaked wool around his heart to delay his death and prolong the suffering. His final words to his disciples were, 'I see the parchment burning, but the letters are flying to heaven' (*Avodah Zarah* 18a).
2. With obvious melancholy on his face.

Bibliography

Sifre to *Dvarim:*

Sifre - ספרי על ספר דברים עם חילופי גרסאות והערות מאת א"א פינקלשטין *on Deuteronomy*, Ed. FINKLESTEIN, L & HOROWITZ, H S, The Jewish Theological Seminary of America, New York and Jerusalem, 1993 (originally published by the Gesellschaft zur Forderung der Wissenschaft des Judentums, Berlin 1939).

ספרי דבי רב עם תוספות מאיר עין - *Sifre debe Rab, der älteste halachische und hagadische Midrasch zu Numeri und Deuteronomium*, Ed. FRIEDMANN, M, Vienna, 1864.

ספרי עם פירוש תולדות אדם מאת הגאון רבי משה דוד אברהם טרו"ש וצ"ל - *Sifre with the commentary Toldot Adam*, Mossad Harav Kook, Jerusalem, 1974. (also includes הגהות גר"א, emendations of the Vilna Gaon).

Sifre - ספרי על ספר דברים בשם עמק הנצי"ב מאת נפתלי צבי יהודה ברלין *with the commentary Emek Han'tsiv*, Jerusalem, (also includes הגהות גר"א, emendations of the Vilna Gaon).

HAMMER, R, *Sifre: A Tannaitic Commentary on the Book of Deuteronomy: Translated from the Hebrew*, Yale University Press, New Haven, 1986.

NEUSNER, J, *Sifre to Deuteronomy, An Analytical Translation* (2 vols), Brown University, Atlanta, 1987.

Tanach:

מקראות גדולות, Pardes Publishing House Inc, New York, 1951,

Ed. COHEN, A, *The Soncino Chumash*, The Soncino Press, NY, 1983.

HERTZ, J, *Pentateuch and Haftorahs*, The Soncino Press, NY, 1987.

HIRSCH, S R, *The Pentateuch, Vol. 5, Deuteronomy, 2nd Ed. (rendered into English by I. LEVY)*, London, 1965.

PLAUT, G W, *The Torah: A Modern Commentary*, UAHC, New York, 1981.

The Jerusalem Bible, Koren Publishers, Jerusalem, 1989.

Ed. SILBERMANN, A, *Pentateuch with Rashi's commentary*, (5 vols), Routledge Kegan Paul Ltd., Jerusalem, 1934.

Rabbinic Texts:

Ed, LIEBERMAN, S, *Tosefta Pe'ah* (Chapters 1 and 4) and *Tosefta K'tubot* (Chapter 6), New York, 1955-1973 (based on MS. Vienna).

Y'rushalmi Pe'ah, (Chapter 8).

Ed. HOFFMAN, D, *Midrasch Tannaim zum Deuteronomium*, Berlin 1908/09, reprinted Jerusalem, 1984.

מכילתא דרבי ישמעאל עם ביאור מרכבת המשנה - *M'chilta d'Rabbi Yishma'el with commentary Mirkevet Hamishneh*, Jerusalem, תשכ"ד.

Sh'mot, Vayikra and *D'varim Rabbah* from:

מדרש רבות עם שני ביאורים ... עץ יוסף וענף יוסף - *Midrash Rabbah* with two commentaries by KOPELOWITZ, Y & KOPELOWITZ, B T, Israel.

מדרש שוחר טוב על תהלים ... עם פירוש מהר"י כהן - *Midrash Shocher Tov on T'hillim* with commentary by COHEN, Y, Jerusalem, תשכ"ח.

Ed. DANBY, H, *The Mishnah*, Oxford University Press, Oxford, 1989.

Talmud (Hebrew Texts from the Vilna-Romm edition as reprinted in the *Soncino Hebrew-English Edition*, The Soncino Press, London, various dates): *Mishnayot; Peah, Shekalim, Shebi'ith, Aboth. G'mara: Sanhedrin, Bava Mezi'a, Berakoth, Ketuboth, Baba Bathra, Gittin, Shebu'oth, Kiddushin.* Minor tractate: *Aboth d'Rabbi Natan.*

GROSSFIELD, B, (Trans.) *The Targum Onkelos to Deuteronomy, The Aramaic Bible Vol. 9*, T & T Clark, Edinburgh, 1988.

Ed. BIRNBAUM, P, *Mishneh Torah*, Hebrew Publishing Co., New York, 1989.

GANZFRIED, S, קצור שלחן ערוך , J. Weinfeld & Co. , Jerusalem.

All translations, unless otherwise stated, are the author's own.

Other texts consulted:

Ecclesiasticus (the Wisdom of Ben Sira), pp.158-251, from, The New English Bible: The Apocrypha, Oxford and Cambridge University Press, 1970.

The Gospel according to St. Matthew, from, *The New Testament in Hebrew and English*, The Society for Distributing the Holy Scriptures to the Jews, London.

Secondary works consulted:

Ed. BARNARVI, E, *An Historical Atlas of the Jewish People*, Hutchinson, London, 1992.

BIRNBAUM, P, *Charity*, pp.520-522, from, *Encyclopedia of Jewish Concepts*, Hebrew Publishing Company, New York, 1979.

BLOCH, A, *Charity*, pp.50-56, from, *A Book of Jewish Ethical Concepts Biblical and Postbiblical*, Ktav Publishing House Inc., 1984.

BOYARIN, D, *Intertextuality and Midrash*, Indiana University, 1990.

BROWN, DRIVER, BRIGGS, *Hebrew English Lexicon of the Old Testament*, Hendrickson, Oxford, 1979.

BRUNS, G L, *Midrash and Allegory: The Beginnings of Scriptural Interpretation*, from, *The Literary Guide to the Bible*, Ed. ALTER, R, KERMODE, F, Collins, 1987.

CARMELL, A, סייעתא לגמא - *Aiding Talmud Study*, Feldheim, New York, 1991.

CASHDAN, E, *Introduction to Aboth d'Rabbi Natan*, Soncino Hebrew-English Ed. Soncino Press, London, 1984.

COHEN, A, *Everyman's Talmud*, Schocken Books, Random House Inc., New York, 1988.

From, Ed. COHEN, A, & MENDES FLOHR, P, *Contemporary Jewish Religious Thought*, Free Press, New York, 1988.
a) FISHBANE, M, *Sacred Text and Canon*, pp.841-847.
b) FISHBANE, M, *Hermeneutics*, pp.353-361.
c) HARTMAN, D & MARX, T, *Charity*, pp.47-54.
d) STERN, D, *Midrash*, pp.613-620.
e) STERN, D, *Aggadah*, pp.7-12.

EISENSTEIN, J, אוצר דינים ומנהגים *(A Digest of Jewish Laws and Customs)*, Israel, 1975.

EPSTEIN, I, *Introductory Essay to Bava Mezi'a*, Soncino Hebrew-English Ed., Soncino Press, London, 1986.

FREEHOP, S B, *Temple Membership and Charity*, pp.175-178, from, *New Reform Responsa*, Hebrew Union College Press, 1980.

GOLDBERG, D, & RAYNER, J, *ch. 6 Under Roman Rule*, pp.73-87, from, *The Jewish People: Their History and Their Religion*, Viking, 1987.

GRANT, M, *The Jews in the Roman World*, Dorset Press, 1984,

HALPERN, J, *History of Our People In Rabbinic Times*, Shapiro Vallentine & Co., London 1948,

HAYMAN, A & HAYMAN A B, תורה הכתובה והמסורה , *Torah Hakethuvah Vehamessurah: A Reference Book of the Scriptural Passages quoted in Talmudic, Midrashic and Early Rabbinic Literature, Part I Pentateuch*, Dvir Publishing Co., Tel Aviv, 1979.

Ed. HOLTZ, B, *Back to the Sources: Reading the Classic Texts*, Summit Books, New York, 1984.

JACOBS, L, *Charity*, pp79-84, from, *What does Judaism say about ...*, Keter Publishing House, Jerusalem, 1988.

JASTROW, M, *Dictionary of the Targumim, Talmud Babli, Yerushalmi and Midrashic Literature*, The Judaica Press Inc., New York, 1989.

LIEBERMAN, *Tosefta Ki-Fshuto: A Comprehensive Commentary on the Tosefta (Hebr.), 8 Vols., Pe'ah*, New York, 1955-73.

LEHRMAN, S M, *Introduction to Shebi'ith*, Soncino Hebrew-English Ed., Soncino Press, 1989.

MACCOBY, H, *Early Rabbinic Writings*, Cambridge University Press, 1990.

MONTEFIORE, C G, & LOEWE, H, *Charity*, pp.412-439, from, *A Rabbinic Anthology*, MacMillan & Co., 1938.

MOORE, G F, *Private and Public Charity*, pp.162-179, from, *Judaism In the First Centuries of the Christian Era: The Age of the Tannaim, Vol. 2*, Harvard University Press, Cambridge, 1950.

POSNER, R P, *Charity*, pp.165-175, from, *Jewish Values*, Keter Publishing House, Jerusalem, 1984 (compiled from material originally published in the *Encyclopedia Judaica*).

RAYNER, J, & HOOKER, B, *Justice, Justice*, pp.88-94, from, *Judaism for Today*, ULPS, 1978.

STEINSALTZ, A, *The Talmud: A Reference Guide*, Random House Inc., 1989.

STRACK, H L, & STEMBERGER, G, *Introduction to the Talmud and Midrash*, T & T Clark, Edinburgh, 1991.

URBACH, E, *The Sages: Their Concepts and Beliefs (The World and Wisdom of the Rabbis of the Talmud)*, Harvard University Press, 1987, (Trans. ABRAHAMS, I).

WEINGREEN, J, *A Practical Grammar for Classical Hebrew, 2nd Ed.*, Clarendon Press, Oxford, 1959.

Encyclopedia Judaica articles, all by HERR, M D,:
Midrash, Midrash Tannaim, Midrashei Halakhah, Sifrei

Notes

This book began life as a paper for my M.A. in Jewish Studies at the Leo Baeck College in London and I am very grateful to the tutors who saw me through that course which led to a qualification that I have put to good use in particular in my activities as a *Sofer STa"M* (scribe), writing and repairing the very words that grace to front cover of this book.

That so much insight into human nature and lessons on how to live properly can be derived from a few short verses in our holy *Torah* has never ceased to amaze me. I hope that this work does justice to some of those insights and lessons and encourages people to actively consider them when they ... GIVE!

About the author

Marc Michaels is the Director of Direct and Relationship Marketing at the Central Office of Information and for well over two decades has been working on social marketing campaigns designed to to save lives, help people find work, claim benefits, avoid substance abuse, live healthier, make proper provision for the future and many others.

In what little spare time he has, as well as his main job, Marc is also a practicing Jewish scribe *(Sofer STa"M)*. This involves writing, and restoration work on, sacred texts written on parchment with a feather quill.

Marc studied under the late Vivian Solomon *z'l* for five years and has an M.A. in Jewish studies from the Leo Baeck Rabbinical College.

His scribal website is at www.sofer.co.uk.

Other books from Kulmus Publishing
(available through www.lulu.com)

Shirat Ha-Olam - The Song of theWorld
ISBN: 978-0-9810947-0-0
Marc Michaels © 2009

Pictures from nature and around the world; words from the Torah, Prophets and Writings. Seventy digitally unaltered photographs matched to an appropriate biblical verse - each with its own story, told in this inspirational book. A feast for the eyes and the mind (149 pages set in a special *sofrut* font and Palantino).

Tikkun Megillat Hashoah
ISBN: 978-0-9810947-1-7
Marc Michaels © 2008

Authorised by the Schechter Institute and the Rabbinic Assembly, this is the *Tikkun* (copyist's guide) for the *Megillat Hashoah* (Holocaust scroll). It contains the full unpointed text in full colour hand-written *STa"M*. It also supplies explanations of the various **visual** *midrashim* and information about how the scroll came to be written and the importance of this new piece of liturgy.

For use by scribes and readers and for Jewish institutions and places of learning.

Packed with many full colour photographs.

Care of Your Torah - A Guide
ISBN: 978-0-9810947-2-4
Marc Michaels © 2008

A short 19 page guide written by a *Sofer STa"M* (scribe) to help Synagogues care for their Torah scrolls. With lots of useful tips and photographs showing many examples of what can make a Torah *pasul* (not kosher).

**The East London Synagogue
- Outpost of Another World**
ISBN: 978-0-9810947-3-1
Marc Michaels © 2008

The East London Synagogue, established 1877 in Rectory Square, Stepney Green, began life as a 'deficit synagogue' against the stated policies of the United Synagogue, who until that time, had only operated on the basis of supporting those communities who would be self financing. Described by the Revd. Joseph Stern as 'a rallying point in this locality' what was the intended role for this 'outpost of another world'? Did it succeed? A short history of the early days of the East London Synagogue, Rectory Square, and an examination of how it came to be established in 1877. With rare photos of the interior of the building taken before its closure. Expanded edition with many more photos. (58 pages).

Thoroughly Modern Moses
ISBN: 978-0-9810947-4-8
Marc Michaels © 2009

Joseph Rosenberg, not so eminent Jewish scientist and time-traveller came to Earth with a bump and was surprised, nay shocked, to learn that he had landed on one of the most famous people in the history of history itself ... Moses the Lawgiver. Ordered to replace Moses by the Lord God Almighty, Supreme Being of the Universe and all round Nice-Guy, Mr. Rosenberg embarks on an adventure of biblical proportions. Will he survive? Will there be tea and cake? A science-fiction biblical comedy. Hitch-hikers meets the Bible - enjoy! (Contains over 300 pages of laughter).